CONTENTS

Introduction	ix
Who is this book for?	x
Background to the approach	x
Global figures	xi
The 4-Pillar framework	xii
—Key elements	xii
—Continual improvement	xv
Chapter 1 Risk Assessment Planning Process	1
Risk planning	1
Structure	2
—Risk mitigation approach questionnaire	3
Chapter 2 Policies and Procedures	9
Gifts, hospitality and expenses	9
Conflicts of interest	9
—Indicators of conflicts of interest	10
—Conflict-of-interest declarations	10
Procedures and fraud risk	10
—Reporting procedures	11
—Reporting guidance	11
Codes of conduct	11
Policies and procedures	12
—Procurement risk questionnaire	13
—Asset management questionnaire	17
—Financial management questionnaire	19
—Security management questionnaire	21
Chapter 3 Building an Anti-corruption Culture	24
Cultural framework	24
Communication barriers	24
Ethical response vs anti-corruption culture	25
Designing out corruption	25
Common corruption barriers	26
Vendor counter-fraud and corruption system	26
Reporting procedures	26
Reporting guidance	26
Connecting strategy to anti-corruption culture	27
Creating a counter-fraud culture	27
—Leadership	28
—Environment	28
Success measurement	29
Communication strategy	29
—Cultural questionnaire	32

Chapter 4 Current Counter-fraud Framework   **35**

Risk mitigation framework   35

   —Risk   37

   —Culture   37

   —Risk reporting   37

   —Compliance structures   37

Chapter 5 Typologies of Procurement Fraud and Corruption   **40**

Defining procurement fraud   40

   —Defining procurement   40

   —Defining fraud   40

Procurement fraud typologies   41

   —Abuse of contract variations or additional works   41

   —Asset misappropriation   41

   —Bid manipulation   41

   —Bid rigging   42

   —Bid rotation   42

   —Bid suppression   42

   —Bribery and corruption   42

   —Cartels   42

   —Complementary (cover) bidding   42

   —Counterfeit products   42

   —Cyber-threat   42

   —Defective pricing   42

   —Diversion of payments   43

   —Email compromise   43

   —False declarations   43

   —False invoicing   43

   —Fictitious vendors   43

   —Ghost/shell companies   43

   —Inflated claims and mischarging   43

   —Market sharing   43

   —Price fixing   44

   —Product substitution   44

   —Purchases for personal use or resale   44

   —Rigged design or specification   44

   —Split purchasing   44

   —Unjustified single/sole source   44

Scope of procurement fraud   44

Elements of procurement fraud   45

   —Pre-contract award risk   46

Insider threat in asset management   55

   —Rental   55

External threat in asset management   55

Corrupt practices   55

How are contract funds diverted or laundered?   56

Procurement corruption and associated money laundering   57

External threats   57

   —Defective pricing   57

   —Overcharging   58

PROCUREMENT FRAUD AND CORRUPTION

How to identify and mitigate procurement fraud and corruption risk

Stephen Tosh

Grosvenor House
Publishing Limited

This book is published by
Grosvenor House Publishing Ltd
Link House
140 The Broadway, Tolworth, Surrey, KT6 7HT.
www.grosvenorhousepublishing.co.uk

A CIP record for this book
is available from the British Library

ISBN 978-1-80381-418-6
eBook ISBN 978-1-80381-419-3

—False claims   58
—Counterfeit products   58
—Diversion of payments   59
—Business email compromise   59

Chapter 6 Organised Crime Groups' Infiltration of Procurement   60
Figures   60
Defining organised crime groups   61
Impact   61
Enablers—why is it made possible?   61
Organisational enablers   62
—Resource   62
—Compliance   62
—Pressure   62
—Demand   62
Defining corruption   62
—Petty corruption   62
—Grand corruption   63
—Political corruption   63
The value of corruption to organised crime groups   63
Organised crime tactics   63
—Bribery   63
—Fraud schemes   63
—Extortion   64
Organised crime illicit activity   64
Corruption within procurement   64
Organised crime supply chain   65
—Manufacture   65
—Transportation   65
—Landlords   66
—Sales   66
Intermediaries   66
Counterfeiting and the links to organised crime   66
How corruption is used   66
Why organised crime groups move into legal business   67
Organised crime proceeds invested in the legitimate economy   67
White-collar crime   68
White-collar crime links to organised crime   68
Cartels   68
Bid rigging and cartels   68
Motivation   68
How criminals infiltrate public procurement   69
Covid-19 use of opportunity   69
Areas targeted   70
Political and personal connections   70
Corruption and the insider threat within procurement   70
—Low-level corruption   70
—Grand corruption   70
Organised crime networks   71
Cartels and corruption   71

Risk indicators within the submission phase 71
Risk indicators within the assessment phase 71
Emerging trends 72

Chapter 7 Risk Areas Within Projects 73
Project planning 73
Project risk framework 74
Project manipulation 74
Project fraud risk 75
—Ad hoc and emergency works 75
—Risk management 76
—Risk reports 76
—Support roles 77
—Project and contract management risk 77
—Bid rigging 78

Chapter 8 Counterfeit Product Risk 81
Terminology 81
Distinguishing counterfeit products 82
—Counterfeit medical products 82
—Counterfeit and substandard pharmaceuticals 82
Law, regulation and legal protection 82
—Trademark 82
—Copyright 82
—Patents 82
—Industrial design 83
—Global impact 83
Counterfeit pharmaceutical mortality rates 83
Impact of counterfeit pharmaceuticals 84
Threat to life 84
Sector impact from counterfeit products 84
Trade in counterfeit and illegal pesticides 85
Trends in trade in counterfeit and pirated goods 85
Global routes 86
Transit nations 86
Global enablers 86
Organisational enablers 87
Process risk factors 87
The use of corruption 87
Forged labels and documents 88

Chapter 9 Data Collection 89
Ability to collect data 89
—Data sources and risk identification 89
—Data analysis 89

Chapter 10 Procurement Fraud Risk Assessment 94
Global themes 94
Value of risk assessments 94
Risk assessment process 95
—Risk planning 95

Risk appetite 96
Assessing culture 98
—Designing out procurement fraud 98
—Partners 99
—Environment 99
—Communication and engagement 99
Vendor counter-fraud system 99

Chapter 11 Risk Assessment Model **100**
Risk model elements 100
Tactical Response 101
Disruption 101
Risk assessment 102
—Implementing 102
—Maintaining 103
—Measuring 103
—Improving 103
Types of risk assessment 103
Individual risk factors 103
Process risk factors 104
Control risk factors 105

Chapter 12 Prevention Approach **106**
Global themes 106
Introduction to risk mitigation 107
Risk mitigation 107
—Causality 107
—The seven c's of fraud risk review 108
Common procurement fraud barriers 109
Common procurement fraud controls 109
—Procurement systems 109
—Security assessment 110
—Internal control component 111
Audit approach 112
Audit triangle 112
Audit control framework 113
Prevention awareness 113
Training and awareness 114
Communicating policy 114
Prevention policy and procedures 114
Financial controls 115
Quality controls 115
Human resources 116
Recruitment process 116
Asset misappropriation controls 117
Asset tracking 118
Vetting controls framework 118
Bid rigging controls 118
Monitoring controls framework 119
Management review 119
Due diligence controls 119

Influencing and manipulating public procurement 120
Risk mitigation approach 120
Organised crime partnership approach 120
Mitigation 121
Supplier onboarding 121
Global counterfeit solutions and technologies 121
Supply chain security 122
Independent external oversight 122
Vendor fraud risk questionnaire 123

Chapter 13 Detection and Data Analysis **125**
Planning 125
Defining the problem 126
Purpose of analysis 126
Data sources 127
Common data analysis 127
Vendor onboarding 127
Tender process 128
Payment process 128
Procurement data 128
Asset management 129
Interpreting data 129
Data compilation 129
Asset misappropriation 129
Data analysis 130
Tender analysis 130
Financial analysis 131
Common risk analysis 131
Detection of counterfeit products 133
—Visual checks 133
—Detection technologies 133
Global response 134
Monitoring schemes 134
Procurement fraud data analysis 136

Chapter 14 Decision-making and Change Management Process **144**
Risk matrix and key recommendations 144
Dedicated compliance group 144
Fraud response plan 145
Monitor and review 147

Chapter 15 Creating a Risk Mitigation Strategy **148**
Designing out procurement fraud 149
—Strategic approach 150
—Anti-counterfeiting 153
—Building a compliance framework 153
—Reporting 154

Acronyms **155**

INTRODUCTION

The typologies and methods of committing corruption and fraud within procurement systems can be diverse in nature and in many respects are only limited by the creativity of those individuals wishing to commit fraud or other financial crime against an organisation's procurement, asset management and financial systems. The conduct and illicit relationships that are created or used to commit fraud are, in many cases, covert in nature, and as such, identifying the fraud and corruption, how it is committed, and individuals' involvement can be challenging. Thus, it can be difficult to mitigate the risk of procurement fraud and corruption completely and is one of the main reasons why a structured approach to identify and prevent procurement fraud should be taken.

Procurement fraud is recognised as one of the biggest financial crimes globally, and bribery and corruption as a facilitator that assists the significant loss to national spend within government procurement. An organisation that doesn't place adequate value on procurement and financial controls, expertise and compliance places itself at an increased risk of being the victim of procurement fraud and corruption. It is only at the point of placing organisational expertise and compliance at the heart of risk mitigation that it will be able to measure more accurately the positive impact and performance of its control measures and counter-fraud and anti-corruption strategy.

When linked to corruption and an insider threat, procurement fraud and other financial crime can undermine national development, good governance and competition, which impacts the lives of the poorest, where monies could have been spent on national growth or other development projects, such as health, education and infrastructure.

Recognising the significant number of risks that can impact an organisation—including roles and people who have the potential to influence or manipulate projects and the procurement life cycle that includes a lack of trained personnel, procurement and financial controls, and compliance measures in place—can undermine the design and implementation of an anti-corruption and procurement fraud approach. Since procurement fraud and corruption continue to develop in scope, scale and creativity, the risks, typologies and routes to mitigation should be regarded as part of a constantly assessed and updated approach.

Creating an anti-corruption and counter procurement fraud approach should provide an awareness of the criminal risks within an organisation's procurement and associated processes and reinforce the importance and vital role of leadership, ethics, professionals and staff in building an anti-corruption culture to protect organisational revenues and reputation.

Individuals working within this environment—whether as leaders or managers, professionals working within compliance, risk, procurement, finance departments or other parts of an organisation that can be impacted by fraud or corruption or are required to introduce prevention-control measures or response to corruption risk—can be hindered by various challenges or competing priorities. These issues can be compounded where an organisation has been the target of procurement fraud or corruption and it is not fully understood how a framework that will identify and prevent future illicit activity can be introduced or updated.

To understand the internal challenges facing an organisation, it may be necessary to ask difficult questions. Is there a lack of expertise within an organisation that could help understand what controls should be in place, or of adequate knowledge and capability to introduce prevention measures or assess the performance of any anti-corruption approach? Do leadership question the cost implications in implementing a compliance programme or the value of an external review of the current anti-corruption approach? Is there a perception by managers that there will be project delays and cost implications of the perceived bureaucracy if a counter procurement fraud programme is introduced, or is this a tactic used by corrupt individuals to influence normal compliance or monitoring processes?

Who is this book for?

This book has been put together to outline the main procurement fraud risks and explain how to assess and introduce mitigation. The design of this approach, which considers available data and how it can be used to continually assess, identify and mitigate procurement fraud risk, can be used by professionals who work in procurement and associated roles, which might include finance, quality assurance, project management and civil engineers.

Professionals working within the compliance or audit fields can increase or refresh their knowledge in this area of expertise, and when considering recommendations for identified risk as part of an organisational review can consider this framework approach to support recommended actions to mitigate current or future risk.

Background to the approach

Having worked in the corruption and procurement fraud environment for over 25 years in various roles and sectors, including the investigation of high-value and complex corruption cases that highlighted the diverse methods in which corruption is used to commit other crimes, such as procurement fraud, what is evident is that investigation alone will not stop corruption occurring again in the future.

The intelligence field in law enforcement taught valuable lessons when it came to the identification of data sources, collection of information on crime risk and the methods in which it can be used to assess risk and introduce a proportionate mitigation response. At an operational level, intelligence can assist in the development of criminal investigations and identify its scale or crime network to support managerial decision making for staff, resources and budgetary requirements, and at a strategic level it can help plan and introduce a long-term response to risk mitigation. This approach can be used in all sectors and be adapted to the size and complexity of an organisation.

It is only the understanding of which data sources can be used to analyse fraud and corruption risk, and the collection of this data, that can help build a risk picture, so that any organisation can more accurately determine its level of risk and plan its approach to prevent future threats.

Having seen the lack of connection between risk identification, investigation and crime prevention within public- and private-sector organisations—including information-sharing and the assessment and review of corruption and procurement fraud risk—meant that many organisations were more likely to have a repeat of these events and methodologies. In 2014 having led the British Standard Working Group to create 'BS10501: Guide to Implementing Procurement Fraud Controls', it became clear that introducing a framework approach to prevent procurement fraud and corruption creates a greater opportunity to identify and mitigate risk.

Using frameworks for assessing methods of preventing procurement fraud and corruption has been an integral part of our approach to risk mitigation, regardless of whether the task was to look at the risk of revenue loss of a specific bribery or fraud suspicion or to provide training to key leadership and management. Taking an assessment approach in all counter-fraud or corruption activities ensures that a framework approach is up to date.

Teaching a framework approach within education programmes and outlining the typologies and fraud and corruption methods, including which areas should be considered to detect and prevent future risk, are powerful tools that have assisted organisations assess and uncover the level of insider threat and gaps in mitigation. These programmes and evaluation methods have helped various organisations introduce capabilities that have included compliance departments and field compliance teams, national training programmes to assist staff reporting on current risks, whistleblower hotlines, and data management departments to collect and assess an organisation's data sources to determine the level of bribery risk and assist national reporting requirements.

In the following chapters a 4-Pillar framework that contains a 16-step approach to identify and prevent corruption and procurement fraud risk is discussed in detail and looks at how to introduce a framework that builds on the foundation of education, data collection, risk assessment and the coordinated response and implementation of a change management process. Planning and following this approach one step at a time, collecting all available data, will additionally assist in assessing the challenges and performance measurement in each area. This information can then be used in later steps when designing a strategic response.

Global figures

In attempting to understand the financial impact that procurement fraud and corruption can have at an organisational or national level, we must first contemplate some of the global estimated figures that have been published.

1. Experian (2017)[1] published its findings on fraud in the United Kingdom and estimated that procurement fraud equates to an estimated £121.4 billion, which is 4.76% of the total expenditure of all sectors. Even if the percentage of fraud is inaccurate, a fraction of this amount still constitutes a significant loss to procurement fraud, and in countries that have larger volumes and values of procurement, or have weaker control measures, there is a likelihood that the percentage of financial loss will be greater.
2. One of the typologies of procurement fraud concerns counterfeit products. The Organisation for Economic Cooperation and Development (OECD)[2] estimates that such products constitute approximately 3.3% of global trade or $590 billion annually.
3. The Department of Justice (DOJ)[3] in the United States of America released its annual report of civil recoveries for fraud and false claims against the US in 2020, showing recoveries of $2.2 billion in settlements and judgements.
4. The International Monetary Fund[4] confirmed that if all countries were to reduce corruption, they could gain $1 trillion in lost tax revenues or 1.25% of global GDP.

---

[1] https://www.experian.co.uk/blogs/latest-thinking/fraud-prevention/fraud-costing-uk-more-than-190bn-released-annual-fraud-indicator/
[2] https://www.oecd-ilibrary.org/trade/trends-in-trade-in-counterfeit-and-pirated-goods_g2g9f533-en
[3] Justice Department Recovers Over $2.2 Billion from False Claims Act Cases in Fiscal Year 2020 | OPA | Department of Justice
[4] https://www.imf.org/external/pubs/ft/fandd/2019/09/the-true-cost-of-global-corruption-mauro.htm

5. The UK National Health Service Counter Fraud Authority estimates that it is vulnerable to £291.4 million worth of procurement and commissioning fraud annually.

6. In 2019 the World Economic Forum confirmed that corruption alone costs developing countries $1.26 trillion every year.

One of the challenges in quantifying these figures is that when you compare—as an example, the annual GDP value of national procurement compared to the national assessment of fraud loss—and then contrast this with detection values, prosecution amounts or financial recovery figures, there is a significant imbalance between estimated loss figures and detection and recovery amounts. If you base the value of a risk mitigation approach purely on the recovery of fraud losses, then in many cases you will likely not receive leadership agreement when the enhancement of a compliance capability is necessary.

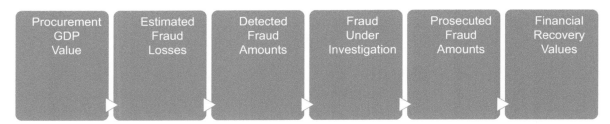

The 4-Pillar framework

There is no one approach that will identify and prevent corruption and procurement fraud risk completely. The investigation and prosecution of allegations may prevent further cases in the short term; however, where organisations and sectors have large spend and significant volumes of procurement, greater emphasis needs to be placed on designing a framework that has a structured and comprehensive approach to risk.

In the 16-step 4-Pillar approach, each step is connected to the next and should be followed as a coordinated methodology. Taking this approach will not only assist in the greater understanding of the typologies of corruption and procurement fraud and where an organisation can be targeted, but will also identify where the weaknesses in the risk framework are.

Identifying and understanding the benefits and the results of each step of the process is an important part of maximising the performance of each step, which will improve the results of the risk assessment, decision-making and change management process.

KEY ELEMENTS

The 16 steps can be broken down into four key elements: risk planning, risk assessment, prevention and detection approach and the change management and performance of the introduced counter-fraud and corruption measures.

Planning

The design of a counter-fraud framework starts with risk planning—specifically, with the assessment of the anti-corruption and procurement fraud structure currently in place within each organisation.

Areas assessed as part of the planning stage start with risk identification, including finance, procurement, security and asset management procedures and the compliance framework currently in place that identifies and prevents fraud and corruption.

The focus on building an anti-corruption culture and community through communication and engagement can help the assessment of an organisation's risk and its ability to enhance its risk identification and prevention approach. This initial planning stage will clarify the framework structure currently in place or whether part of an external audit can be used to assess the health of an organisation's counter procurement fraud framework.

Risk Assessment

Identification of risk is an essential part of developing an organisational and national risk profile. Training on the typologies of corruption and their links to fraud and other financial crime is an important part of risk identification and preventing corruption.

Understanding which internal data sources can be used to profile risk within each organisation, and whether this information can be accessed, centrally collated and analysed, will help build a more accurate risk assessment.

To create an efficient and effective process that assists regular and ongoing assessment of risk, constructing a risk model that outlines relevant areas to be considered—including individuals, departments and stakeholders understanding their role and responsibility within the framework—is integral.

Prevention and Detection Approach

Documenting the risks identified as part of the risk assessment process is the starting point in introducing a decision-making and change management process. Having a regular or continual process of detection through data analysis and audit can help identify areas of risk and assist in the monitoring and enhancement of control measures.

Introducing a central decision-making group of leaders and managers to respond to identified risks, help enhance a change management process and promote transformation into an anti-corruption culture can make a significant impact.

Change management

Introducing a formal process of individual and department responsibilities for a coordinated response where fraud or corruption risk is identified is an important part of an effective and cohesive risk mitigation framework.

Using a strategic approach to risk and an organisation's anti-corruption framework supports long-term planning and a continual improvement process.

Collecting data to monitor and measure the performance of an counter-fraud framework is an important part of continual improvement. Introducing training and awareness as part of continual learning and introducing awareness where new risks are identified ensures a greater opportunity to identify risks and gaps in an approach to risk.

STEP	APPROACH	BENEFITS & RESULTS
RISK PLANNING		
Step 1	Anti-corruption approach questionnaire	Documenting initial assessment of gaps in policies and procedures, expertise and capability, and systems and controls
Step 2	Policies and procedures	Documenting current policies and procedures, including procurement, payment, asset management, security, quality assurance and counter-fraud
Step 3	Anti-corruption culture (communication and engagement)	Proactive communication and engagement can act as a prevention approach by sending a strong zero-tolerance counter-fraud and corruption message
Step 4	Health check and framework	Documenting steps 1 and 2 and gaps in the current approach, which can be used as the foundation of building the anti-corruption framework
RISK ASSESSMENT		
Step 5	Typologies	Training and assessment of the typologies of corruption and their links to fraud will assist in understanding how and where an organisation can be targeted
Step 6	Ability to collect data	Recognising the internal and external data sources that can be used to detect and profile areas of risk
Step 7	Risk assessment and profile	Building a profile of current risks will assist year-on-year measurement and identification of new risks, which will assist response and change management
Step 8	Risk assessment model	Identifying stakeholders and structures of engagement, including outputs required to build a strategic response
PREVENTION & DETECTION		
Step 9	Risk register and risk matrix	Documenting and monitoring risks that can be used in reporting and a change management process
Step 10	Prevention measures	Assessment of common control measures that should be in place to mitigate risk, including finance, procurement and compliance
Step 11	Detection measures	Methods and techniques used to detect risk or control weakness
Step 12	Designated compliance group	Decision-making and change management group implemented to introduce a coordinated response where suspicions of procurement fraud are identified
CHANGE MANAGEMENT		
Step 13	Corruption response plan	Document ownership and responsibility of leadership and management in decision-making and change management process
Step 14	Corruption & procurement fraud strategy	Design of a strategic approach and long-term planning in response to the risk assessment
Step 15	Measuring and monitoring	Assessing the performance of your framework, which includes increased reporting, data collection, training, risk identification and non-compliance
Step 16	Training and awareness	To enhance and repeat the framework process, improving knowledge of new risks and reporting and prevention methods

CONTINUAL IMPROVEMENT

The 4-Pillar approach is not a one-off activity but should be a process that is under regular or continual review and is used as a process designed around an annual risk assessment. The framework is designed so that it can be used to continually improve an organisation's approach to risk and its identification and implementation of control measures.

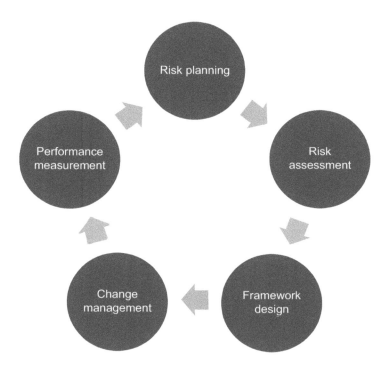

CHAPTER 1
Risk Assessment Planning Process

Designing an organisation's approach and response to risk is an essential process in preventing procurement fraud and corruption. However, before taking the first step towards introducing a risk assessment process, taking stock of current policies and procedures, expertise, capability, and systems and controls in place is an important part of understanding the current framework in place and an organisation's approach to risk.

Once there is a documented picture of what is in place, you can then move to the next pillar in your approach of risk identification. Being able to compare a risk assessment against current control measures and compliance programmes will assist you to identify gaps in the current approach to risk and consider the measures that should be introduced to identify and prevent future corruption and fraud once a risk assessment has been concluded. The planning process is integral to the successful identification of risk and to introducing the correct controls and mitigation response.

Risk planning

Before any risk assessment can be carried out that might include the review of future projects, understanding what should be assessed and risks that can be considered must be introduced into the planning process. This process is necessary to design and build the structure of a risk framework to assess the people, process and control risks—specifically, who can influence or manipulate the procurement or payment processes—organisational control weaknesses or individuals who may be the target of bribery.

A planning process should be instigated and staffed by suitably qualified personnel. Its purpose is to set out the parameters of the risk assessment process and areas to be reviewed, along with a process of documenting risks and recommendations that update and enhance the current risk framework.

Key staff who will lead, coordinate and implement the risk framework should also be identified within each organisation. This will support the overall coordinated approach and implementation of the organisational or national risk framework, including the ongoing risk assessment process.

One of the risks regularly seen when reviewing organisations is that when interviewing the leadership team about organisational policy and procedures, they tend to quote what the policies and procedures are, and not what happens in practice, either because they want to give an impression of compliance—that they know what is going on—or they don't see the importance of counter procurement fraud or the potential or actual financial impact. Therefore, to understand the differences between what is documented and how it is implemented in practice, it is important to interview staff who work in departments that implement policy and procedures. This will give greater clarity to compliance concerns, gaps in control measures and how they can be manipulated or influenced.

Structure

At the planning stage, to assess how the current framework is implemented across an organisation, where applicable, the following information must first be identified and understood. This includes:

1. size and structure of an organisation, including country and international operations
2. activities of the organisation
3. supply chain and asset management structure
4. type and scale of project activity
5. procure-to-pay data management process
6. an organisation's ability to collect, analyse and disseminate data
7. the current counter procurement fraud framework in place
8. an organisation's ability to introduce a procurement fraud risk framework across all relevant areas
9. the ability to assess risk and identify gaps in the organisational risk framework

The focus of an initial assessment will depend on what has been introduced as part of an organisation's procedures and compliance programmes. However, areas that should be assessed as part of the planning process might include:

1. procurement and financial procedures and control measures
2. compliance and counter-fraud policies and procedures
3. asset management procedures
4. physical and ICT security procedures
5. quality assurance, including procedures for product and equipment failures

The below risk mitigation approach questionnaire is not intended to be a complete list of checks to identify and prevent corruption and procurement fraud risk but is a starting point for areas to consider as part of an initial assessment of the counter-fraud approach in the planning process. Once answered, the information can then be used to map out the current framework and approach to fraud and corruption risk.

RISK MITIGATION APPROACH QUESTIONNAIRE

PLANNING

Does the organisation have an anti-corruption policy?	☐ Yes	☐ No
Do you have appropriately qualified personnel to conduct a risk assessment to identify which activities or other aspects of the organisation's business have corruption risk?	☐ Yes	☐ No
Does the organisation have identified anti-corruption stakeholders with defined roles, responsibilities and expectations?	☐ Yes	☐ No
Does the organisation have an anti-corruption response and control measures?	☐ Yes	☐ No
To what extent have an anti-corruption responses and control measures been implemented by the organisation?		
Is there a documented anti-corruption strategy?	☐ Yes	☐ No
Has the organisation designed and implemented a corruption risk framework to meet organisational requirements?	☐ Yes	☐ No
Does the organisation have a continuous improvement cycle?	☐ Yes	☐ No
Does the organisation have an anti-corruption review process?	☐ Yes	☐ No
Has the organisation conducted an anti-corruption review?	☐ Yes	☐ No
Describe the organisation's review processes for anti-corruption policies, procedures, systems and controls and expertise, capability and management structure, including agreed intervals.		
Does the organisation have funding to plan, implement, monitor and review corruption risk and controls?	☐ Yes	☐ No
Does the organisation have personnel to plan, implement, monitor and review corruption risk and controls?	☐ Yes	☐ No
Does the organisation have equipment and materials to plan, implement, monitor and review corruption risk and controls?	☐ Yes	☐ No
Are all internal and outsourced staff who are to be involved in the procurement process subject to appropriate background checks (e.g. financial checks, confirmation of identity, referee checks, conflicts of interest and criminal record checks)?	☐ Yes	☐ No
Does the organisation have a procurement card policy and are these processes transparent and auditable?	☐ Yes	☐ No
Are bribery and corruption risk documented in the organisational risk register and reported to the audit committee?	☐ Yes	☐ No
Comments:		

ASSESSMENT OF RISK

Are there procedures in place to assess the risk of corruption to its existing and proposed procurement and supply chain activities?	☐ Yes	☐ No
Are there procedures in place to assess whether policies, procedures and controls are adequate to mitigate corruption risk?	☐ Yes	☐ No
Is the timing and frequency of risk assessments defined by the organisation?	☐ Yes	☐ No
Are you able to define who within the organisation, including projects, can influence the procurement process?	☐ Yes	☐ No

Is the organisation able to identify, retain, collect and analyse its own sources of data to assess the level of risk?	☐ Yes	☐ No
Does the organisation have an anti-corruption plan and strategy?	☐ Yes	☐ No
Are the organisation's anti-corruption plans, policies, procedures and strategies adequately communicated?	☐ Yes	☐ No
Is adequate due diligence conducted on all suppliers?	☐ Yes	☐ No
Has a review been conducted of control risk areas within the purchasing process (life cycle), including business requirement (i.e. identification of need through to end of life and disposal of assets)?	☐ Yes	☐ No
Is action taken against any breach of the procurement process or related internal policies by staff who work in risk areas?	☐ Yes	☐ No
Is information recorded and centrally held where there has been a breach of policy or procedure?	☐ Yes	☐ No
Are performance bonuses, performance targets and other incentivising elements and remuneration reviewed to ensure that there are reasonable safeguards to prevent these from encouraging bribery?	☐ Yes	☐ No
Is there an end-to-end corruption risk review conducted within projects and how is it documented?	☐ Yes	☐ No
Comments:		

SCOPE OF CONTROLS

What bribery and corruption controls does the organisation have in place with new and existing suppliers?		
What controls does the organisation have in place to ensure that it can purchase materials and services of the required quality, in the correct quantity and delivered to the right place at the right time from a legitimate source at an appropriate price?		
What processes are in place to test the anti-corruption controls to ascertain whether they are sufficient and being consistently applied?		
What procurement and other controls does the organisation have in place to mitigate the risk of the organisation, its personnel or others acting on its behalf committing bribery?		
Does the organisation have adequate financial controls?	☐ Yes	☐ No
What financial controls does the organisation have in place to mitigate the risk of the organisation, its personnel or its suppliers committing or being a victim of bribery or corruption?		
Does the organisation monitor supplier compliance with quality-assurance requirements, which might indicate the provision of poor-quality goods, works or services or product substitution?	☐ Yes	☐ No
Does the organisation have auditable records that accurately document quality assurance?	☐ Yes	☐ No
Is particular attention given to those who have influence over the procurement process or access to financial information at a higher-than-usual level?	☐ Yes	☐ No

Does the organisation conduct no-notice audits as part of the procurement fraud and corruption controls where there is a specific area of risk within an organisation?	☐ Yes	☐ No
How are significant matters identified within audit reports, including any recommended corrective actions or improvements reported?		
Is this information centrally held and response coordinated?	☐ Yes	☐ No
Comments:		

COMMUNICATING POLICY & CULTURE

Has top management communicated that they and the organisation have adopted an anti-corruption policy and controls?	☐ Yes	☐ No
Has this statement and policy been communicated to all the organisation's personnel and suppliers and been published on the organisation's intranet and public website?	☐ Yes	☐ No
What procedures does the organisation have that ensure that all appropriate and relevant personnel receive applicable guidance on business ethics, corporate governance or similar?		
Does the organisation have a corruption or procurement fraud response plan?	☐ Yes	☐ No
Does the organisation have a conflict-of-interest policy?	☐ Yes	☐ No
Does the organisation have procedures that provide that conditions of employment require personnel to comply with ethics and anti-corruption policies?	☐ Yes	☐ No
Comments:		

TRAINING & AWARENESS

Does the organisation have adequate and regular anti-corruption training that includes up-to-date risk and methods of mitigation?	☐ Yes	☐ No
What education, training and awareness does the organisation provide its staff who are responsible for implementing the procurement and anti-corruption controls or who could encounter bribery or corruption as part of their duties?		
Is anti-corruption training and awareness provided to suppliers?	☐ Yes	☐ No
Does the training cover corruption indicators, risks, response plans, reporting and awareness of the organisation's anti-corruption controls?	☐ Yes	☐ No
Has the organisation produced and issued guidance on its procurement methods and controls to staff who might be involved in the procurement process?	☐ Yes	☐ No
Comment:		

LEADERSHIP & MANAGEMENT		
What resources does the organisation use to implement procurement and anti-corruption controls, including personnel, funding and equipment?		
Is the anti-corruption policy approved by top management?	☐ Yes	☐ No
Does top management receive and review information about the content and operation of the organisation's anti-bribery management system?	☐ Yes	☐ No
Who is responsible for the management of compliance with procurement and anti-corruption controls? This person (people) should oversee the implementation/management of the procurement system.		
Is vetting of individuals upon promotion or moving to higher-risk positions conducted?	☐ Yes	☐ No
Comments:		

REPORTING PROCEDURES		
What procedures does the organisation have that enable personnel to report attempted, suspected or actual bribery or corruption, or any breach or weakness within the procurement or anti-corruption controls, to the appropriate person within the organisation (either directly or through an appropriate third party)?		
Does the organisation have processes and procedures that ensure as far as possible that the organisation protects the identity of personnel who make confidential reports?	☐ Yes	☐ No
Does the organisation have procedures that allow anonymous reporting (if, and to the extent that, applicable laws allow)?	☐ Yes	☐ No
Does the organisation have procedures that protect from retaliation personnel who raise in good faith a concern about actual or suspected bribery and corruption or the effectiveness of controls?	☐ Yes	☐ No
Does the organisation have procedures that encourage personnel to seek advice from an appropriate person on what to do if faced with a concern or situation that could involve bribery or corruption?	☐ Yes	☐ No
Does the organisation have procedures that provide clear guidance to personnel on how to raise a concern about attempted, suspected or actual bribery and corruption or the implementation of anti-corruption controls?	☐ Yes	☐ No
Does the organisation have procedures that provide clear guidance to personnel on how and when they can report to appropriate external authorities?	☐ Yes	☐ No
Comments:		

DUE DILIGENCE		
Is adequate due diligence conducted on potential vendors to confirm their ability to provide the works or services specified?	☐ Yes	☐ No
Are conflict-of-interest checks conducted on vendors against staff and suppliers?	☐ Yes	☐ No
Are there documented procedures to undertake enhanced due diligence on a supplier prior to entering any business relationship with it where a risk assessment shows that a supplier might pose an unacceptable bribery or corruption risk?	☐ Yes	☐ No

Does the organisation have in place a method of assessing each vendor against the organisation's procurement standards before placing them on the approved supplier list?	☐ Yes	☐ No
Does the organisation have a defined method and timescale for requalifying companies on the approved supplier list?	☐ Yes	☐ No
Do supplier visiting procedures determine the level of controls a vendor has in place to mitigate bribery risk?	☐ Yes	☐ No
Is there a method of assessing each supplier against the organisation's bribery and corruption standards to ensure they don't carry a known or unknown bribery risk and are able to protect procurement and project revenues?	☐ Yes	☐ No
Comments:		

RESPONSE

Does the organisation publish procedures in which there is a methodical response to allegations or suspicions of bribery or corruption, with defined responsibilities within a response plan?	☐ Yes	☐ No
Is this plan made available to all staff so that they understand their role and responsibilities when bribery or corruption is suspected or identified?	☐ Yes	☐ No
Does the organisation review and update its response plan from lessons learned following a bribery or corruption allegation or investigation?	☐ Yes	☐ No
Does the organisation have procedures that provide for investigation of allegations or suspicions, or any breach or weakness identified within the procurement controls?	☐ Yes	☐ No
Does the organisation have a compliance manager and a mechanism through which they can monitor purchases made by the organisation to confirm compliance with procurement procedures and policies?	☐ Yes	☐ No
Does the compliance manager have in place a mechanism through which they can record and report deviations from laid down policies and procedures and ensure that remedial actions are taken?	☐ Yes	☐ No
Does the compliance manager report, at planned intervals, to top management on the adequacy and implementation of the bribery and corruption controls?	☐ Yes	☐ No
Are audit reports detailing any significant matters identified, and are any recommended corrective actions or improvements provided to the compliance manager and top management?	☐ Yes	☐ No
To ensure the objectivity and impartiality of the audit programme, does the organisation, so far as is reasonable, ensure that the audit is undertaken by an independent function or person within the organisation established or appointed for this process?	☐ Yes	☐ No
To ensure the continuing adequacy and effectiveness of the anti-corruption controls, does top management review the scope and implementation of the procurement fraud controls?	☐ Yes	☐ No
Does the organisation have an information management process to ensure that all material collected from procurement controls and anti-corruption controls that highlight inadequacy or risk management within the procurement process is communicated by top management and to relevant staff to respond to the risk?	☐ Yes	☐ No

Does the organisation have a procedure for changing or improving the controls whenever this is necessary or desirable following compliance management or top management review?	☐ Yes	☐ No
Comments:		

CHAPTER 2
Policies and Procedures

Assessing current policies and procedures—including counter-fraud and anti-corruption—and their compliance by staff and suppliers is an important part of determining if there are gaps in the current mitigation structure. Identifying how non-compliance with policies and procedures can be associated with fraud or corruption risk, how they can be manipulated or whether there are gaps in current policies and procedures that can assist fraud and corruption are valuable approaches to consider when assessing or responding to identified risk. Additionally, introducing a requirement to document an individual's non-compliance with laid down policies and procedures can be a valuable way of collecting additional data on fraud risk that when linked with other data may help identify suspicions of procurement fraud and corruption.

Gifts, hospitality and expenses

It is recognised that the offering of gifts and hospitality can be a route in which bribery is used to obtain or retain contracts. Compliance with procedures is not only introduced to mitigate the risk of bribery but additionally to protect staff and suppliers from being drawn into an investigation or dispute where allegations of misconduct are made. The introduction of transparent and documented procedures to control the extent and frequency of gifts and hospitality is an important step, either through a total prohibition on all gifts and hospitality or by introducing procedures that limit and justify the requirement by reference to:

1. maximum expenditure
2. frequency (relatively small gifts and hospitality can accumulate to a large amount if repeated)
3. the timing of when gifts and hospitality can be given (e.g. not during the tender process or negotiations, nor prior to contract renewal)
4. the reasonableness of giving or receiving gifts, taking into account the market and seniority of the giver or receiver
5. the identity of the recipient, particularly if high risk (e.g. those in a position to award contracts or approve permits, certificates, payments or investigation outcomes)
6. the legal and regulatory environment (some territories and organisations may have prohibitions or controls in place)
7. the requirement for approval in advance of gifts and hospitality above a defined value or frequency by an appropriate manager
8. the requirement for gifts and hospitality above a defined value or frequency to be effectively documented and transparent (e.g. in a register or accounts ledger) and to be auditable

Conflicts of interest

Individual risk factors, where an individual has a personal or financial interest with a vendor, can cause a conflict of interest to arise. In most areas of the procurement life cycle, individual influence has the potential to manipulate the award of a contract or post-award contract management. To understand how conflicts of interest can impact an organisation, we must first consider examples of the various types of risk.

1. Nepotism—granting favours to family in a commercial or political setting.
2. Outside employment or company interests—relatives linked to a bidding company.

3. Cronyism—a friend appointed to a well-paid post regardless of their ability to do the role.

4. Tribalism—loyalty to a tribe, that in some cases can be incompatible with government, where individuals are loyal first to a tribe then a country. Corruption risk can emanate where individuals feel duty-bound to award contracts to their tribe regardless of ability.

5. Revolving door—the movement of individuals between public and private sectors where conflicts of interest or corruption risk can ensue.

6. Sponsorship—for individual or business or organisational activities that may make individuals feel indebted to respond in kind.

7. Agents and their use can be a valuable tool in developing business. However, in many cases an individual's personal or close relationship with executives, decision makers or individuals who influence the award of a contract can create a conflict of interest or corruption risk.

8. Gifts and hospitality given by a current contractor or new vendor outside of the current norms, or policy that might be excessive or not linked to developing ethical business relations.

9. Private interests that may include political donations.

INDICATORS OF CONFLICTS OF INTEREST

Additional verification is always required where there is disclosure or indication of a conflict of interest to prove beyond reasonable doubt the level of confirmed personal or professional relationships. There are several common indicators such as:

1. unexplained or unusual favouritism of a particular contractor or vendor
2. contracting or purchasing employee lives beyond means
3. the employee having discussions about employment with a current or prospective supplier
4. close socialisation with and acceptance of inappropriate gifts, travel or entertainment from a supplier, or not recording gratuity in local registers

CONFLICT-OF-INTEREST DECLARATIONS

To support a counter-fraud culture and strategy, it is suggested that staff in roles that can influence the procurement process should sign an annual declaration that they have no conflicts of interest, or where they have, that it has been documented in accordance with organisational procedures. This type of declaration is also valuable for individuals involved in the tender selection and award process to remind individuals of their compliance and disclosure responsibility.

Procedures and fraud risk

Dependent of the size, the structure and the policies and procedures that have been introduced for the management of an organisation, additional areas, where relevant, that should be considered when assessing fraud and bribery risk, their compliance and audit should include:

1. recruitment and due diligence procedures
2. sales remuneration
3. facilitation request guidance and reporting procedures
4. political and charity donations and contributions
5. the use of business credit cards or procurement cards
6. cash account management

REPORTING PROCEDURES

Building an counter-fraud culture and the internal and external communication and engagement with staff, suppliers and partners can assist the enhancement of an organisation's procurement fraud risk profile. In addition to implementing internal reporting procedures, it should also introduce procedures that encourage and facilitate external reporting by existing or potential suppliers or members of the public. When introducing a reporting point where internal and external reports can be received, an organisation should also implement procedures that:

1. enable individuals to report attempted, suspected or actual procurement fraud and corruption or any breach or weakness within the procurement or fraud controls to an appropriate person within the organisation
2. ensure, directly or through an appropriate third party, that the organisation protects the identity of personnel who make confidential reports
3. allow anonymous reporting and protection from retaliation for personnel who raise in good faith concerns about actual or suspected procurement fraud or the effectiveness of controls
4. encourage personnel to seek advice from an appropriate person on what to do if faced with a concern or situation that could involve procurement fraud

REPORTING GUIDANCE

To support its counter-fraud culture, an organisation should provide clear guidance to its personnel and, where appropriate, its partners and suppliers:

1. on how to raise a concern about attempted, suspected or actual procurement fraud or non-compliance with procurement or other controls
2. assuring them that their reports will be investigated and acted upon and that feedback will be given where appropriate
3. on how to access independent advice
4. on how and when they can report to appropriate external authorities

The organisation should advise personnel of the:

1. ethical responsibility to report any suspected risk of procurement fraud—including a legal duty to report fraud—and the consequences of any breach of this legal duty
2. fact that they will not be at risk of retaliation from the organisation for raising in good faith concern about suspected or actual procurement fraud or implementation of procurement or procurement fraud controls
3. fact that their identity will be protected and kept confidential

Retaliation against someone who in good faith raises a concern about actual or suspected procurement fraud or the implementation of controls should be highlighted as a disciplinary matter, and any such contact may have serious implications, including loss of employment.

Codes of conduct

Publishing codes of conduct or an ethics policy outlines the standards that are expected from staff. Annual sign-off by staff that they have read, understand and will comply with policies can be a useful tool in reminding staff of the zero tolerance to fraud and corruption.

Policies and procedures

The activities of an organisation will also determine the policies and procedures that should be published and followed. Procedures such as procurement, finance, asset management, security and quality assurance should be introduced. When formalising its procedures, an organisation should:

1. publish them and make them available to staff who manage or in some way are involved in the procedure
2. have compliance or monitoring procedures in place
3. have a review process in place where non-compliance is identified or where there are gaps in the procedure

To assist the initial review process and assess the current risk framework in place, several questionnaires are documented below to support the review process.

PROCUREMENT RISK QUESTIONNAIRE

IDENTIFICATION OF NEED		
Was the work invented or needed?	☐ Yes	☐ No
Can the individual raising the identification of need be identified?	☐ Yes	☐ No
Is the requirement falsified or is the work already covered within an existing contract?	☐ Yes	☐ No
Has work been raised outside of the procurement process?	☐ Yes	☐ No
JUSTIFICATION & BUSINESS CASE		
Has the end-user created a business case or requisition that is authorised?	☐ Yes	☐ No
Are there instances where the person who creates the business case raises the requisition and sources the suppliers?	☐ Yes	☐ No
Can procurement staff be engaged without submission of a requisition?	☐ Yes	☐ No
Is the person who identified the business requirement identified within the business case?	☐ Yes	☐ No
DESIGN & SPECIFICATION		
Is the scope of work or design biased towards a specific company's capability?	☐ Yes	☐ No
Is specification reviewed and authorised by someone other than the author?	☐ Yes	☐ No
Is the specification/scope of work vague?	☐ Yes	☐ No
Are specifications independently checked?	☐ Yes	☐ No
BUDGET & COST ESTIMATION		
Has a market price check been conducted and retained?	☐ Yes	☐ No
Is total cost ownership missed within cost estimation?	☐ Yes	☐ No
Is there a lack of budgetary or cost control and management throughout the life of the contract?	☐ Yes	☐ No
Has project funding been split between budgets to hide the true cost of completion?	☐ Yes	☐ No
PROCUREMENT ROUTE		
Is there a documented single source justification and authorisation process and is it followed?	☐ Yes	☐ No
Are procurement decisions documented and open to review?	☐ Yes	☐ No
Can orders be split to avoid the tender threshold?	☐ Yes	☐ No
Have the goods, works or services been single sourced before?	☐ Yes	☐ No
VENDOR IDENTIFICATION		
Does the end-user identify who the bidding companies should be?	☐ Yes	☐ No
Does the organisation have sufficient vendors within the supplier database?	☐ Yes	☐ No
Is the vendor identification process dealt with by the procurement department?	☐ Yes	☐ No
Can vendor identification and procurement routes be influenced by the senior executive?	☐ Yes	☐ No

PRE-QUALIFICATION		
Is suitable financial evidence provided to confirm the supplier's ability to complete the contract?	☐ Yes	☐ No
Are checks conducted to confirm the vendor's ability to perform a contract to specification?	☐ Yes	☐ No
Is there evidence of supplier control systems to manage procurement and procurement fraud and corruption risk?	☐ Yes	☐ No
Does the supplier have a system in place to identify and rectify quality and counterfeit risk within their supply chain?	☐ Yes	☐ No
BID RESPONSE		
Is all communication within the bidding process transparent and shared with all bidding companies?	☐ Yes	☐ No
Are there enough qualified vendors identified to bid for the requirement?	☐ Yes	☐ No
Are response deadlines long enough to prevent manipulation of the bidding process?	☐ Yes	☐ No
Is the bidding process secure and auditable?	☐ Yes	☐ No
TENDER MATRIX		
Is there a scoring matrix that is relevant, objective, measurable and impartial to the requirement?	☐ Yes	☐ No
Can additional criteria be added during the selection process?	☐ Yes	☐ No
Is the scoring mechanism standardised?	☐ Yes	☐ No
Does the organisation have auditable records that accurately document quality assurance?	☐ Yes	☐ No
TENDER SELECTION		
Are there dual controls for opening bids and recording individuals' details?	☐ Yes	☐ No
Is the disqualification of a bidding company justified and documented?	☐ Yes	☐ No
Are persons involved in the selection process required to record conflicts of interest?	☐ Yes	☐ No
Is security within the bidding and selection process tested?	☐ Yes	☐ No
CONTRACT AWARD		
Did the work start before the contract was awarded or the order was raised?	☐ Yes	☐ No
Is work sub-contracted to companies that do not have the required qualifications?	☐ Yes	☐ No
Is work sub-contracted to a company that was involved in the initial bid?	☐ Yes	☐ No
Is the award process transparent and documented?	☐ Yes	☐ No
AD HOC & EMERGENCY WORKS		
Is there an excessive number of ad hoc or emergency works?	☐ Yes	☐ No
Is there a documented process for ad hoc or emergency works?	☐ Yes	☐ No
Is there root cause analysis conducted to establish reasons for emergency works?	☐ Yes	☐ No
Is there a procedure to confirm that works are required and completed?	☐ Yes	☐ No

CONTRACT VARIATIONS		
How soon after mobilisation is the first variation requested?	☐ Yes	☐ No
Is there a process of identifying and monitoring a high percentage of variations compared to original costs?	☐ Yes	☐ No
Are variations caused by inadequate design and specification during the planning stage?	☐ Yes	☐ No
Is fraud risk assessment considered as part of the variations process, including root cause analysis?	☐ Yes	☐ No
SIGN-OFF		
Can one person identify a need and sign off work as complete?	☐ Yes	☐ No
Are there documented procedures to verify work as complete?	☐ Yes	☐ No
Are contractors' hours checked against timesheets and onsite verification of attendance?	☐ Yes	☐ No
Are scarce resources, such as civil engineers and project managers, monitored for procurement fraud risk?	☐ Yes	☐ No
ASSET MANAGEMENT		
Are there security procedures and risk assessments in place for warehouses and assets in transit?	☐ Yes	☐ No
Do assets procured have a goods receipt and are they documented on the asset register?	☐ Yes	☐ No
Are losses of high value and attractive or high-volume items monitored?	☐ Yes	☐ No
Are variance reports monitored, with no automatic adjustments before fraud risk is mitigated?	☐ Yes	☐ No
PROJECT MANAGEMENT		
Are fraud risks assessed for each stage of the project?	☐ Yes	☐ No
Is data held and monitored for actual costs against budget or forecast costs?	☐ Yes	☐ No
Do contractors have adequate counter-fraud procedures in place?	☐ Yes	☐ No
Is there adequate site management for delivery and project sign-off?	☐ Yes	☐ No
SUB-CONTRACTING		
Are sub-contractors authorised before use?	☐ Yes	☐ No
Are conflict-of-interest checks carried out on sub-contractor companies?	☐ Yes	☐ No
Can it be confirmed that sub-contractors were not part of the tender process?	☐ Yes	☐ No
Have normal vetting procedures been conducted to ensure the sub-contractor is not a ghost company?	☐ Yes	☐ No
FALSE CLAIMS		
Is the process of comparing requisition, purchase order and invoice carried out before payment is made?	☐ Yes	☐ No
Is a goods-receipt note received and goods placed on an asset register before payment?	☐ Yes	☐ No
Is there a process in place to check for inflated invoices and double billing?	☐ Yes	☐ No
Is there evidence of non-delivery of goods?	☐ Yes	☐ No

CONTRACT MANAGEMENT		
Is there evidence of regular equipment failures?	☐ Yes	☐ No
Is work carried out after hours or at weekends, when there is no supervision?	☐ Yes	☐ No
Is there a field compliance team to verify the completion of works to correct specifications?	☐ Yes	☐ No
Is there evidence of deliberate delays in the project to incur additional costs, including rental of equipment?	☐ Yes	☐ No
Comments:		

ASSET MANAGEMENT QUESTIONNAIRE

WAREHOUSE		
Is there a process for delivery-note receipt and retention?	☐ Yes	☐ No
Are procured goods placed on the asset register?	☐ Yes	☐ No
Are checks conducted and reports generated for loss of assets?	☐ Yes	☐ No
Is the total value of assets missing/lost/stolen documented?	☐ Yes	☐ No
Do the assets procured balance with assets recorded on the electronic asset register?	☐ Yes	☐ No
Is there evidence of non-delivery?	☐ Yes	☐ No
Can quantities of non-delivery items be measured?	☐ Yes	☐ No
DISPOSAL OF ASSETS		
Is the sale of goods for disposal conducted through competition?	☐ Yes	☐ No
Is there a laid down procedure and authorisation process for disposal of assets?	☐ Yes	☐ No
Are there laid down procedures to prevent asset loss?	☐ Yes	☐ No
Is the sale of assets conducted through auction?	☐ Yes	☐ No
Is there evidence that goods are devalued to facilitate supplier profit?	☐ Yes	☐ No
Is the weight of disposed metals decreased to facilitate a higher profit by the vendor?	☐ Yes	☐ No
Is there evidence of weighbridge inoperative having to use supplier capability?	☐ Yes	☐ No
Is there evidence that good-quality materials are signed off as scrap?	☐ Yes	☐ No
Are conflicts of interest checks carried out on individuals involved in the disposal process?	☐ Yes	☐ No
Are companies involved in the purchase of disposal goods suppliers of the same goods?	☐ Yes	☐ No
Are disposal companies connected to manipulate disposal price?	☐ Yes	☐ No
Is there evidence of the sale of disposal material for cash rather than electronic transfer or destruction?	☐ Yes	☐ No
Are there adequate security systems in place to monitor the storage and disposal of assets?	☐ Yes	☐ No
Can the same employee identify, approve and dispose of scrapped goods or obsolete inventory?	☐ Yes	☐ No
Can an employee who initiated or authorised the disposal of materials record or authorise the inventory adjustment?	☐ Yes	☐ No
Are there controls between the sale, invoicing and payment receipt for disposal materials?	☐ Yes	☐ No
Is there a method of analysing the level of write-offs?	☐ Yes	☐ No
Can assets be disposed of without authorisation?	☐ Yes	☐ No
Is there a significant increase in damaged assets?	☐ Yes	☐ No

MATERIAL MANAGEMENT		
Are employees who receive goods from vendors also involved in the purchasing?	☐ Yes	☐ No
Are employees who receive goods able to record invoices within the procurement system?	☐ Yes	☐ No
Is there independent review of physical inventory?	☐ Yes	☐ No
Are there controls in place to prevent manipulation of inventory records?	☐ Yes	☐ No
Are there controls in place to prevent unauthorised write-offs?	☐ Yes	☐ No
Is there adequate investigation prior to any authorised write-off?	☐ Yes	☐ No
Can one employee initiate, authorise and record a manual adjustment within the inventory system?	☐ Yes	☐ No
Is there evidence of incorrect quantities within the goods receipt note?	☐ Yes	☐ No
Does the organisation have a process of recording movement of materials?	☐ Yes	☐ No
Is there a correct level of long-lead items to prevent delay and additional costs?	☐ Yes	☐ No
Is there a process for disposal of items that have reached the end of their shelf life?	☐ Yes	☐ No
Is this process auditable (i.e. for theft of attractive items)?	☐ Yes	☐ No
GOODS RECEIPT		
Is there a goods receipt note that links the receipt, recording and delivery of goods?	☐ Yes	☐ No
Can the organisation link its procurement activity to an asset register?	☐ Yes	☐ No
Can the person who creates the need take receipt of the goods?	☐ Yes	☐ No
Is the receipt of goods reconciled with the warehouse inventory?	☐ Yes	☐ No
Are there security procedures and risk assessments in place for warehouse and assets in transit?	☐ Yes	☐ No
Are losses of attractive, high-value or high-volume items monitored?	☐ Yes	☐ No
Are variance reports monitored and no automatic adjustments made before fraud risk is mitigated?	☐ Yes	☐ No
Comments:		

FINANCIAL MANAGEMENT QUESTIONNAIRE

DUAL CONTROLS		
Are there dual controls in changing payment details?	☐ Yes	☐ No
Are there dual controls in amending supplier details?	☐ Yes	☐ No
Are there dual controls in adding or deleting suppliers?	☐ Yes	☐ No
Is access to the accounts payable department restricted?	☐ Yes	☐ No
Can account details be amended without dual controls?	☐ Yes	☐ No
Can one person have the authority to manage budgets, procure and make payments?	☐ Yes	☐ No
FINANCIAL CONTROLS		
Is there adequate segregation of duties in financial controls?	☐ Yes	☐ No
Is there transparency and accuracy in the financial data?	☐ Yes	☐ No
Are advanced payments used for non-urgent requirements?	☐ Yes	☐ No
Is there consistent data analysis of financial information for fraud risk?	☐ Yes	☐ No
Is total cost ownership missed within cost estimation?	☐ Yes	☐ No
Are financial systems audited for incomplete or erroneous data?	☐ Yes	☐ No
Are there regular audits and strict management controls of financial approval limit authority or of misusing delegations?	☐ Yes	☐ No
BUDGETS		
Are there procedures for the adoption of budgets?	☐ Yes	☐ No
Is there evidence of payments being allocated to cost centres not linked to projects?	☐ Yes	☐ No
Is reporting of expenditure accurate and timely?	☐ Yes	☐ No
Are there audit procedures in place?	☐ Yes	☐ No
PAYMENT PROCESS		
Is there a payment authorisation process?	☐ Yes	☐ No
Is there a process for monitoring overpayments?	☐ Yes	☐ No
Is there a process in place to monitor double billing for the same item?	☐ Yes	☐ No
Is delivery of materials confirmed through goods receipt notes before payment is made?	☐ Yes	☐ No
Are goods recorded on an asset register before payment is made?	☐ Yes	☐ No
Is there a significant number of invoices received when material hasn't been delivered?	☐ Yes	☐ No
Is there a significant number of invoices received without a purchase order?	☐ Yes	☐ No
Are three-way checks conducted before payment is made?	☐ Yes	☐ No
Are invoices checked against contract pricing schedules?	☐ Yes	☐ No
What is the finance departments response when a purchase order isn't referenced on an invoice?		
Are invoices received from suppliers without a purchase order reference?	☐ Yes	☐ No

Are the works or services detailed in the invoice verified as complete before payment is made?	☐ Yes	☐ No
Are invoices in the expected format?	☐ Yes	☐ No
Are the invoiced goods, works or services information detailed correctly?	☐ Yes	☐ No
Is pricing information retained and monitored for significant price increase?	☐ Yes	☐ No
CASH MANAGEMENT		
Does the organisation have a documented system for handling cash?	☐ Yes	☐ No
Are handling and storage procedures audited to confirm security within cash management?	☐ Yes	☐ No
Are there adequate segregation of duties in cash handling, receipt and deposit?	☐ Yes	☐ No
Are there anomalies between cash receipt and deposit?	☐ Yes	☐ No
Are there situations where cash is used to pay for low-value contracts?	☐ Yes	☐ No
Comments:		

SECURITY MANAGEMENT QUESTIONNAIRE

POLICY & PROCEDURE		
Has a level of security been implemented that is informed by a risk assessment to protect all data from unauthorised access and disclosure?	☐ Yes	☐ No
Does the organisation restrict access to master vendor data, including tender quotes, unit pricing, competitive bids, or any other data, to authorised persons who need to have access for the purposes of fulfilling their role?	☐ Yes	☐ No
Does the organisation have guidance in place to ensure data are processed in a secure manner?	☐ Yes	☐ No
Does the organisation have an audit capability within IT systems to monitor the dissemination of data?	☐ Yes	☐ No
Can you define the segregation of duties throughout the procurement life cycle, including the tendering process, procure-to-pay and contract management?	☐ Yes	☐ No
Is there a security policy?	☐ Yes	☐ No
Does the whistleblower policy cover the protection of data and identity of individuals?	☐ Yes	☐ No
Is there a clear desk policy?	☐ Yes	☐ No
Are there reporting procedures so that security concerns are recorded and reported?	☐ Yes	☐ No
Are there warehouse security procedures?	☐ Yes	☐ No
Is there a contractual clause with staff and suppliers to protect company data?	☐ Yes	☐ No
Is there a security review or audit of security procedures?	☐ Yes	☐ No
Is particular attention given to those who have influence over the procurement process or access to financial information at a higher-than-usual level?	☐ Yes	☐ No
Is action taken to any breach of the procurement process or related internal policies by staff who work in risk areas?	☐ Yes	☐ No
Does the organisation have a person designated as responsible for supply chain security, with defined responsibilities and sufficient authority to drive forward recommendations?	☐ Yes	☐ No
Does the designated person through communication and staff training ensure that internal and external controls and procedures provide the necessary security?	☐ Yes	☐ No
How does the organisation determine the level of supply chain security within its operations? This might include manufacture, handling, storage and transportation, including loading and unloading.		
Comments:		

TENDER SECURITY		
Is the tender box held in a secure location?	☐ Yes	☐ No
Are there procedures for opening the tender box (minimum two persons) and recording bid submissions?	☐ Yes	☐ No
Are the details of the individuals opening the bids recorded?	☐ Yes	☐ No
Are there conflict-of-interest checks conducted for individuals involved in the tender board?	☐ Yes	☐ No
EMAIL SECURITY		
Are secure email addresses used for receiving vendor bids?	☐ Yes	☐ No
Are late bids automatically rejected within the email system?	☐ Yes	☐ No
Are there email controls in place to minimise unauthorised disclosure of commercial data?	☐ Yes	☐ No
Is supplier registration and commercial data handled securely to prevent unauthorised disclosure to competitors?	☐ Yes	☐ No
Does the email system have an audit solution in place?	☐ Yes	☐ No
ICT SECURITY		
Is there an IT policy and security marking to restrict the dissemination of sensitive data?	☐ Yes	☐ No
Are permissions removed when an individual moves companies or departments?	☐ Yes	☐ No
Is commercial data restricted on a secure server?	☐ Yes	☐ No
Do temporary staff have restricted access to IT system?	☐ Yes	☐ No
Does the IT system have an audit capability?	☐ Yes	☐ No
Are there dual controls to add or remove supplier from system?	☐ Yes	☐ No
PHYSICAL SECURITY		
Are there physical security measures does the organisation have that are designed to prevent unauthorised access to equipment, installations, material and data?	☐ Yes	☐ No
What physical security measures does the organisation have that are designed to safeguard against unauthorised removal or dissemination of data?		
Does the organisation have physical security measures in place to prevent unauthorised access to or tampering with back-up data?	☐ Yes	☐ No
What segregation of duties does the organisation have within the functions throughout the procurement life cycle, including the tendering process, procurement to pay and contract management?		
Does the organisation link all procurement activity to an asset register?	☐ Yes	☐ No
Is access to procurement and finance departments restricted to authorised personnel only?	☐ Yes	☐ No
Are all vendor visits authorised and recorded?	☐ Yes	☐ No
Are there warehouse internal and external security procedures?	☐ Yes	☐ No

Are contract files held within secure storage and have in/out procedures?	☐ Yes	☐ No
Is there secure storage and handling procedures for archived contract files?	☐ Yes	☐ No
Is access restricted to temporary staff?	☐ Yes	☐ No
Are segregation of duties introduced in purchasing, receipt, vendor selection and payment roles?	☐ Yes	☐ No
Comments:		

CHAPTER 3
Building an Anti-corruption Culture

In the same way that any culture is introduced and developed within an organisation to mitigate risk—whether it is health and safety, ethics or a culture of continuous learning, where consistent measurement is introduced to assess individual performance against laid down standards or how an individual understands their role and responsibility with this approach—creating an counter-fraud and anti-corruption culture in many respects is no different.

Building an anti-corruption culture is not just about focusing on the insider threat and how to deter a member of staff from committing corruption, but it is engaging all areas of a business or organisation in introducing or reinforcing values, principles and behaviours. In assessing an organisation's culture, are there rituals or consistent and repeated actions that build its culture and are standards based on ethics? And in developing its culture, is there continual learning and is knowledge shared and integrated into an organisation's anti-corruption approach?

Each individual, whether they are staff, partners, consultants, suppliers or other stakeholders, should understand through an organisation's communication that it takes fraud, corruption and the protection of its revenues and reputation seriously. This would include the implications should fraud or corruption be identified.

Cultural framework

In initiating an approach to introduce or enhance a counter-fraud and anti-corruption culture, there are elements in this framework that should be examined:

1. Publishing the standards that are expected for all individuals, suppliers and partners that work in or with the organisation.
2. Building a knowledge base and sharing information on organisational standards, policy, leadership and anti-corruption messages and activities, including training and awareness.
3. Ensuring that staff members are actively engaged in building the culture of an organisation and that a mapping exercise is conducted of its activities and external engagement to identify individuals or organisations to support and build the anti-corruption culture.
4. Continuous assessment and improvement of an anti-corruption approach, which might include measuring staff confidence or opinions of organisational culture through questionnaires or surveys.
5. Communication linking all areas discussed through verbal, written and flow of information that coordinates the communication strategy and enhances the anti-corruption culture.

Communication barriers

There are common themes globally where an anti-corruption culture is limited or non-existent because of the actions or attitudes within an organisation. Some of these themes include the following:

1. A board and executive where there is no anti-corruption message from the CEO or the board to set the tone and culture for the organisation.

2. Although an organisation may have an anti-corruption policy, if it doesn't have engagement and communication with staff, partners and suppliers, it limits the development of an anti-corruption culture and the opportunity to identify corruption risk.

3. The lack of internal and external communication with staff, partners and suppliers may give the appearance that an organisation isn't serious about risk mitigation and may make it a bigger target for corruption and procurement fraud.

4. Where an organisation doesn't have education as part of its risk mitigation strategy, it is likely to restrict the opportunity for staff to recognise, identify and report procurement fraud.

5. A lack of engagement or communication with staff and suppliers limits the opportunity for risk identification and reporting of corruption suspicions.

6. Staff are unaware of an organisation's anti-corruption policy or do not trust the organisation's response when it comes to protecting a company's reputation or implementing a proper governance response to incidents of corruption.

Ethical response vs anti-corruption culture

There can be occasions where an organisation's ethical response doesn't match its view or perception of its anti-corruption culture. Challenges might include the following:

1. Where an organisation's ethical response doesn't match what it aspires to achieve in creating an anti-corruption culture, then it is unlikely that an organisation will be able to build a sustainable anti-corruption culture.

2. Where there is evidence of improper conduct or poor performance in dealing with ethical issues, an unethical culture or behaviour is likely to be tolerated. Examples of such behaviour might include:

    a. reporting ethical issues through line management that aren't addressed
    b. whistleblower reports not being appropriately dealt with, and an individual being targeted by the organisation through bullying, intimidation or other improper actions
    c. improper treatment of suppliers
    d. using conflicts of interest or corrupt activities when obtaining or retaining contracts

Designing out corruption

Communicating an anti-corruption message can have a positive impact on an organisation's approach to reduce crime against it. An approach that several global proactive initiatives take to prevent crime is communicating a strong and consistent message that an organisation takes corruption and procurement fraud seriously and persons intent on committing these offences stand a greater likelihood of getting caught. Given the actual or perceived view that this is likely to happen, there is a greater opportunity to reduce corruption and financial loss from internal and external sources because it makes individuals think twice about committing crime.

When building an anti-corruption culture, areas that should be considered when creating an organisation's response may include:

1. assessing for an insider threat and the governance structures and activities in place, including the communications strategy that informs staff and consultants that the organisation takes corruption seriously

2. the external threat, including communication and engagement with suppliers, so that they understand and support the counter-fraud culture and confirm the action they're taking and make clear the actions and response the organisation is taking to protect its revenues

3. partner and supplier engagement including building anti-corruption relationships that ensure procurement fraud or bribery risk isn't passed on, including information sharing on known or new fraud and bribery methods

Common corruption barriers

Proactive action within an organisation's control measures communicates a strong message to vendors on how serious an organisation is about detecting fraud, corruption and associated financial crime risk. Common barriers include:

1. having a robust supplier onboarding process that includes confirming conflicts of interest, identifying politically exposed persons (PEPs) and communicating organisational ethics policies
2. introducing contract clauses that cover bribery and corruption, competition and unethical behaviour within the lifetime of the contract
3. publishing and communicating procurement, financial and quality-assurance control measures
4. an organisation's ability to receive and respond to reports of suspicious activity
5. communicating compliance procedures to prevent improper relationships with suppliers
6. testing the integrity of the compliance system for corruption risk

Vendor counter-fraud and corruption system

To communicate an organisation's values and counter-fraud and corruption culture as part of the onboarding process, clarification should be sought from the vendor of their action in the following areas, including:

1. evidence of their counter-fraud and governance programmes, including the involvement and engagement by its leadership team in identifying and mitigating procurement fraud and corruption risk
2. evidence of a vendor's risk management system showing that a vendor assesses its fraud, corruption and bribery risk and that they can mitigate passing potential risks onto their clients
3. the vendor having anti-corruption policies, codes of conduct and can evidence that it is published internally and publicly
4. the vendor providing counter procurement fraud and bribery training for their staff and suppliers, and if not, that they are agreeable to receive your training before future business engagements
5. there being staff engagement in developing the vendor's anti-corruption initiatives and that they have a published hotline and helpline information to provide guidance on ethics concerns

Reporting procedures

In building an ethics culture and enhancing the risk profile of an organisation, introducing an environment where staff, suppliers and members of the public feel safe when reporting ethical concerns—knowing that they will be taken seriously—can increase the number of reports and ultimately lead to a greater understanding of an organisation's procurement fraud risk.

Reporting guidance

To support the counter-fraud culture, an organisation should provide clear guidance to personnel and its suppliers on how to raise a concern about attempted, suspected or actual procurement fraud or the implementation of procurement or compliance controls.

Connecting strategy to anti-corruption culture

The design of a risk mitigation approach can differ between each organisation and is dependent on several factors, including the size of the organisation, the countries and sectors in which it operates, its commercial activities and supply chain and the number of suppliers. To reinforce an organisation's culture and its approach to risk, there are six areas that you should be communicated.

1. Prevention and the message and activities communicated in all aspects of an organisation's business, including controls, policies and procedures, compliance structures and activities.
2. Communicating the seriousness an organisation places on detecting fraud and corruption and what its response will be where procurement fraud and corruption is detected, or communicating non-compliance with organisational control measures or policies and procedures.
3. Financial recovery and having a structure in place where organisational losses are identified and recovered through commercial, civil or criminal law. Also, publishing this information within contracts to inform suppliers about action that might be taken should fraud be identified.
4. Introducing policies and communicating activities—such as limiting timescales in high-risk positions and movement of staff—to reduce the risk of bribery and corruption.
5. Investigation is the reactive part of the strategy, where suspicious activity is identified and action is taken to understand the level of illicit behaviour and whether legal action is required. Publishing concluded investigations can be used as part of a prevention approach when communicated to staff and suppliers.
6. Publishing sanctions that are available to an organisation to deter current or future misconduct from individuals or organisations, which may be introduced where contractual or compliance requirements are deliberately breached.

Creating a counter-fraud culture

The foundation of an organisation's mitigation strategy is an organisation's counter-fraud and corruption culture, which is created and incorporated within the DNA of all staff. In developing an organisation's culture, two areas of focus should include communication and engagement with all individuals and organisations who can have a positive impact on the change management process.

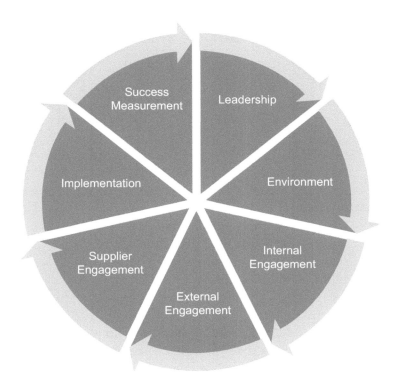

LEADERSHIP

To set an example for organisational values, practices and behaviours expected of all individuals, leadership should engage and communicate their expectations and responsibilities.

1. Ownership and responsibility are critical to the success of any counter-fraud culture and communication strategy ensuring its implementation and ongoing development.
2. The tone from the top—including communication—which includes setting an ethical example for the organisation and the anti-corruption message communicating the organisational values to staff and suppliers.
3. Publishing policy and procedures, which should include an annual reminder and sign-off of conflict-of-interest and ethics policies, that should be communicated to all staff.
4. Creating and publishing a counter-fraud and corruption strategy, including organisational structure and response to known risks.
5. The executive and board should be briefed on the performance of counter-fraud and corruption efforts and culture.
6. Leadership's review of counter-fraud and corruption control measures.

ENVIRONMENT

The environment and approach to facilitate communication and engagement within an organisation should consider a number of basic elements.

1. Regular and honest communication, including the ability for staff and suppliers to report concerns freely.
2. The reporting process should be clear and published so that all staff recognise where to report their concerns. In detecting fraud, hotlines are globally recognised as one of the main ways in which fraud and corruption are identified.
3. A whistleblower protection policy is an important part of promoting an organisation's integrity and the seriousness it places on receiving reports of suspected criminality and the support that is available to staff who come forward.
4. Education and awareness are part of the foundation of a communication strategy in ensuring that staff understand the breadth of fraud and corruption typologies, where an organisation can be targeted and their role in recognising, reporting and responding to suspicious activity.

Internal engagement

To build a culture and an environment of transparency, communication and engagement with staff, putting staff in the driving seat should be considered and might include:

1. counter-fraud forums that include sharing current fraud and corruption themes, building interest and capability within an organisation, identifying experience and their experiences of corruption and associated financial crime risk, and discussing control or culture weaknesses, including opportunities to mitigate risk
2. a centralised ethics platform that can serve in the coordination and communication of counter-fraud efforts, particularly where several departments are involved in the implementation of the counter-fraud strategy
3. having a central library within the ethics platform that can assist in the coordination of counter-fraud and corruption efforts through the publication of policies, procedures and the counter-fraud message
4. questionnaires and feedback that can be used in various aspects of the strategy, including developing the counter-fraud capability, identifying gaps in organisational response, better engagement with staff and suppliers or the effectiveness of training and awareness programmes

Supplier engagement

Communicating an organisation's counter-fraud and anti-corruption approach, engaging suppliers and building supplier relationships can be opportunities to enhance an organisation's response to corruption and reinforce its anti-corruption culture. Such communication might include the following:

1. Contract clauses including anti-corruption and anti-bribery, competition and conflicts of interest—they are a message to vendors of the zero-tolerance and reporting mechanisms where fraud and corruption are suspected or identified.
2. Supplier briefing—a valuable tool in enforcing your organisation's stance on procurement fraud or corruption. Updating suppliers on current fraud and corruption threats and methodologies can act as a preventative and proactive response in risk mitigation.
3. The reporting process—a useful tool within the bidding and contract award procedures or within the contract management of large projects where irregularity is identified.
4. Accountability and responsibility, including how an organisation responds when fraud or corruption suspicions are identified—an important part of communicating that an organisation is serious in dealing with these issues.

External engagement

In many locations, including international environments, there can be great value in communicating with and engaging externally, which might include individuals and organisations, to promote and build your anti-corruption message and culture.

1. External communication through different media to suppliers, partners and the public reinforces an organisation's anti-corruption stance.
2. Involvement with local, national or international organisations that support the development of an organisations anti-corruption culture.
3. Actively engaging in local or national anti-corruption forums or creating forums to understand local issues or share and develop best practice.

Success measurement

Measuring an organisation's activities that support their counter-fraud strategy and culture is integral to continuous improvement and understanding the current challenges and positive or negative changes within an organisation.

1. Measurement and performance indicators are essential in monitoring and reporting the positive outputs of the strategy, including additional planning where negative outcomes—including non-compliance with policies—are identified.
2. Data collection and ensuring that an organisation has access to all its data sources and has opportunities for individuals to report fraud and corruption risk through internal and external hotlines.
3. Continuous improvement and monitoring of the performance of the communication strategy and its benefits to the organisation is essential to the ongoing development and success of the strategy.

Communication strategy

In some respects, many of the areas in the communication strategy are obvious. However, when introduced together they send a strong message to staff, partners and suppliers that an organisation is serious about their counter-fraud approach and mitigating risk that could be transferred from other organisations.

To enhance the culture of an organisation requires the coordinated formation of a communication strategy that builds on various aspects of an organisation's intention to engage all staff, partners, suppliers and stakeholders in its drive to identify and mitigate risk. When planning a communication strategy and developing an organisation's culture, several areas should be considered.

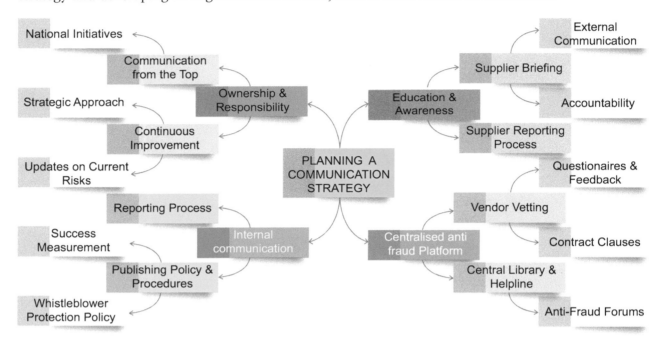

1. **Ownership** and **responsibility** are critical to the success of any communication strategy ensuring that the implementation and ongoing development of the procurement fraud and anti-corruption policy is coordinated and consistent.
2. Communication from the chief executive and setting an example, including a statement of the organisation's **values,** to staff and suppliers is an important part of the fraud and corruption prevention message. Where there is no message from a senior executive, there may be occasions where individuals do not trust their line management or organisation to deal with their suspicions correctly. In these situations, an organisation may miss out on fraud and corruption reports, and that limits their understanding of the risk their organisation faces.
3. **Continuous improvement** and **monitoring** of the performance of its culture and its benefits to the organisation is essential to the ongoing development and success of the strategy.
4. Success **measurement** and **performance indicators**—including additional planning and change management where negative outcomes are identified—are key to monitoring and reporting the positive outputs and successes of the counter-fraud and corruption culture. Do staff or suppliers trust an organisation's integrity and that they will deal with their reports without any reprisal? What is the level of staff engagement? And is there an increase in reporting that is linked to increased engagement or training of staff?
5. **Regular** and **honest communication**—for instance, the ability for staff to report concerns, including areas of an organisation's risk mitigation, that can be introduced or improved—is an important part of engagement and staff involvement in building a counter-fraud culture where staff can see the results of their suggestions.
6. A reporting process should be clear and published so that all individuals recognise the process and where to report their concerns. **Hotlines** are globally recognised as one of the key methods in which fraud and corruption is detected. Organisations should consider both internal and external reporting lines; however, they should monitor the reporting process for fictitious or malicious reports.

7. Publishing and communicating counter-fraud and corruption **policies and procedures**, including an annual reminder to all staff of the requirement to sign conflict-of-interest declarations and ethics policies.

8. A **whistleblower protection policy** plays an important part in highlighting an organisation's integrity, the seriousness it places on receiving reports on suspected criminality and the support that is available to protect staff who come forward and disclose in good faith from retaliation or unethical conduct.

9. A **centralised counter-fraud platform** can serve in the coordination of risk mitigation efforts, particularly where several departments are involved in the communication and implementation of the strategy.

10. Having a central **library** within a counter-fraud platform additionally assists in the coordination of counter-fraud efforts and awareness.

11. **External communication** through different media to suppliers, partners and the public reinforces the counter-fraud and proactive stance of the organisation.

12. **Questionnaires** and **feedback** can be used in various aspects of a strategy, including developing the counter-fraud capability, procedures and controls. This process can include feedback or surveys from staff working in different areas of an organisation's culture, and communication that might include training programmes, staff engagement and the effectiveness and security of its hotline.

13. **Contract clauses** that communicate to suppliers the position taken toward fraud and corruption and the consequences should there be a breach during the lifetime of the contract. This might include counter-fraud, anti-bribery, competition and conflict-of-interest clauses, all of which are a key message to vendors of the zero-tolerance and reporting mechanisms where fraud or corruption is suspected or identified.

14. Counter-fraud **forums** can be an important part of sharing current fraud themes and building interest and capability within an organisation. Engaging staff from various backgrounds and departments within an organisation can assist in the greater understanding of the gaps in an organisation's anti-corruption or compliance approach.

15. **Education** and **awareness** are part of the foundation of a communication strategy in ensuring that staff understand the breadth of procurement fraud risk and their role within the organisation in recognising and responding to suspicious activity. The Association of Certified Fraud Examiners[5] in its Report to the Nations confirmed that tips are more likely to be received through hotlines when an organisation has received counter-fraud training and are more likely to be detected where training is in place.

16. **Supplier briefing** can be a valuable tool in communicating the importance the organisation places on procurement fraud risk mitigation and informing suppliers of current threats, which can act as a preventative and proactive response in coordinating counter-fraud activity.

17. A **supplier reporting** process can be a useful tool within the bidding and award process and within large projects, where many contractors can be engaged in fraudulent activity.

18. **Accountability** and **responsibility**—including how an organisation responds when fraud suspicions are identified—are important parts of communicating that an organisation is serious in dealing with fraud.

Although the questionnaire highlights some of the areas that should be considered in building an organisation's culture, it should also be measured alongside other areas of business risk—specifically, security, finance, procurement, asset management and quality assurance. There is limited value in having a strong counter-fraud culture when an organisation has poor internal controls.

---

[5] 2020 ACFE Report to the Nations

CULTURAL QUESTIONNAIRE

LEADERSHIP

Does the CEO/board publish an anti-corruption message and policy?	☐ Yes	☐ No
Does the organisation identify and publish who is the owner of the organisation's anti-corruption culture and response?	☐ Yes	☐ No
Does the CEO/board set a consistent ethical example?	☐ Yes	☐ No
Are ethics and conflict-of-interest policies signed off by staff annually?	☐ Yes	☐ No
Does leadership create and publish an anti-corruption strategy, including organisational structure and response to known risks?	☐ Yes	☐ No
Is the CEO/board briefed on the performance of the anti-corruption approach and culture?	☐ Yes	☐ No
Does leadership implement the organisation's reviews to assess anti-corruption controls?	☐ Yes	☐ No
Comments:		

COMMUNICATION

Does the organisation have regular and honest anti-corruption communication with staff and suppliers?	☐ Yes	☐ No
Does the organisation actively promote its ethics/corruption- and fraud-reporting hotline internally and externally?	☐ Yes	☐ No
Does the organisation publish its whistleblower policy to staff and suppliers?	☐ Yes	☐ No
Is education and awareness part of an organisation's anti-corruption culture?	☐ Yes	☐ No
Comments:		

INTERNAL ENGAGEMENT

Does the organisation engage its staff in its anti-corruption efforts?	☐ Yes	☐ No
Does the organisation have a centralised platform to coordinate anti-corruption and fraud communication and efforts?	☐ Yes	☐ No
Does the organisation have a centralised library for anti-corruption and fraud knowledge sharing?	☐ Yes	☐ No
Does the organisation engage with staff to identify gaps in anti-corruption efforts?	☐ Yes	☐ No
Comments:		

SUPPLIER ENGAGEMENT		
Are counter-fraud, bribery, competition and conflict-of-interest clauses used within all contracts?	☐ Yes	☐ No
Does the contract contain an counter-fraud message (zero tolerance), including reporting hotline information?	☐ Yes	☐ No
Are suppliers briefed on the types of fraud the organisation is identifying?	☐ Yes	☐ No
Do suppliers receive anti-corruption or procurement fraud training prior to engagement?	☐ Yes	☐ No
Comments:		

EXTERNAL ENGAGEMENT		
Is external communication used to reinforce the organisation's anti-corruption stance?	☐ Yes	☐ No
Is the organisation involved with external organisations to develop anti-corruption and counter fraud culture?	☐ Yes	☐ No
Is the organisation actively engaged in anti-corruption and fraud forums to understand local and national issues?	☐ Yes	☐ No
Comments:		

SUCCESS MEASUREMENT		
Are performance indicators used to measure development of counter-fraud culture?	☐ Yes	☐ No
Are all internal data sources available to measure the level of the organisation's risk?	☐ Yes	☐ No
Are the organisation's anti-corruption and procurement fraud efforts monitored to continuously improve culture?	☐ Yes	☐ No
Comments:		

COMMUNICATING POLICY & PROGRAMME		
Has top management communicated that they and the organisation have adopted an anti-corruption policy and controls?	☐ Yes	☐ No
Has this statement and policy been communicated to all the organisation's personnel and suppliers and been published on the organisation's intranet and public website?	☐ Yes	☐ No
What procedures does the organisation have to ensure that all appropriate and relevant personnel receive applicable guidance on business ethics and corporate governance?		
Does the organisation have a published corruption and procurement fraud response plan?	☐ Yes	☐ No

Is the conflict-of-interest policy and register communicated and available to all staff?	☐ Yes	☐ No
Does the organisation have procedures that provide conditions of employment and require personnel to comply with ethics, anti-corruption or procurement fraud policies?	☐ Yes	☐ No
Comments:		

TRAINING & AWARENESS		
Does the organisation have adequate and regular corruption and procurement fraud training that includes up-to-date risks, methods of mitigation and organisational policies and procedures?	☐ Yes	☐ No
What education, training and awareness does the organisation provide to its staff who are responsible for implementing the procurement, corruption and compliance controls, or who could encounter corruption as part of their duties?		
Does the training cover procurement fraud indicators, risks, response plans, reporting and awareness of the organisation's procurement fraud and corruption controls?	☐ Yes	☐ No
Has the organisation produced and issued guidance on its procurement methods and controls to staff who might be involved in the procurement process?	☐ Yes	☐ No
Comments:		

CHAPTER 4
Current Counter-fraud Framework

The final step of the planning process is to document the identified risks and map out the current counter-fraud and corruption, business and compliance structures that are in place. Once complete, this step will add value to the risk assessment process and document the fragmented nature of the framework and approach to countering procurement fraud.

This approach can be a valuable tool, particularly in large organisations where departments or business areas have been the target of procurement fraud or corruption. Each organisation may have a different approach and framework structure, and listing risks and mapping out the current counter-fraud framework gives an organisation the opportunity to assess, at a glance, key areas of the approach, which will enable it to assess information flow that supports the assessment of risk and how this information can be introduced into the decision-making and change management process.

In addition to the overall risk mitigation approach, this risk planning method can also be used for several purposes:

1. As an external assessment of an organisation's approach to risk.
2. As part of an approach by procurement regulators when reviewing risk mitigation prior to its approval of new projects.
3. In the identification of the root cause of procurement fraud where systems and control measures are manipulated.

Documenting the purpose of the framework and what outcomes you wish to achieve can help the design of your approach to risk identification and mitigation.

Risk mitigation framework

Mapping out this structure will help individuals involved in the decision-making and change management process visualise the current approach and assess whether it meets the prevention requirements of the risks identified in the planning process from the completed assessment questionnaires. In designing an organisation's mitigation approach, areas that could be considered include:

1. a central decision-making and change management group and a structure where reported fraud suspicions are responded to
2. a reporting process to communicate with the risk committee, executive or board on specific risks that may impact the organisation
3. how new information is used and how it can be added to the risk assessment and the mitigation structure, which includes an operational risk assessment, risk picture, risk identification and mitigation framework, and the strategic response
4. compliance or risk mitigation structures, including the adequacy or effectiveness of expertise and capability, policies and procedures, and systems and controls
5. the activities of a counter-fraud culture, including internal and external communication and engagement

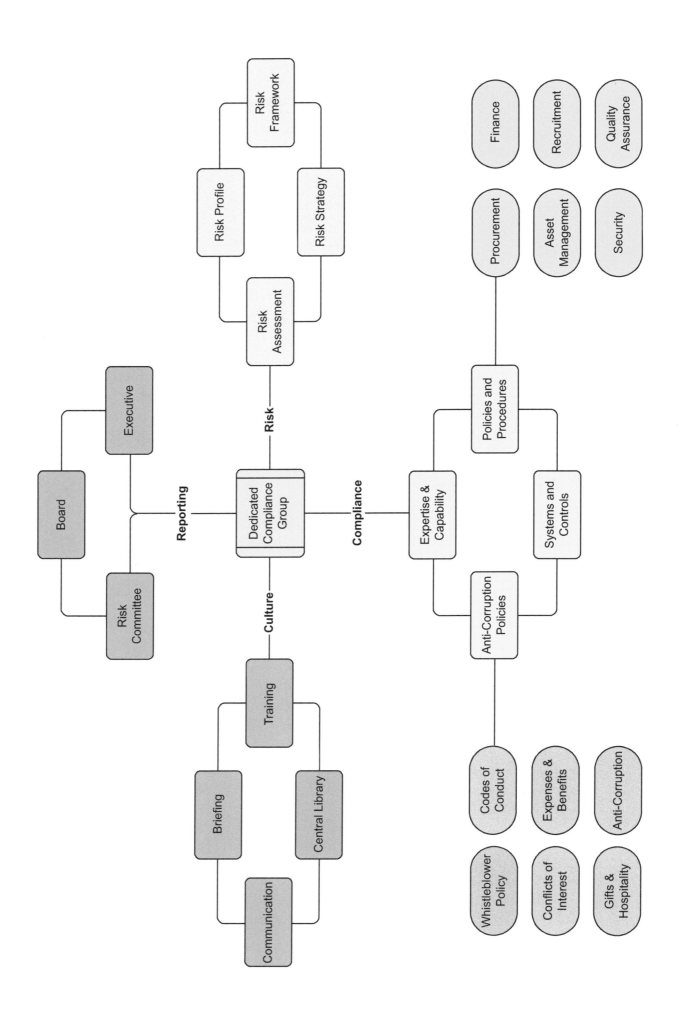

RISK

Reviewing how data is used operationally, tactically and strategically to help understand and respond to procurement fraud risk is a useful process in confirming the risk identification and mitigation approach.

1. Risk Profile
   Operational and tactical assessments—created from available risk information—that assist a specific investigation or an assessment of risks that impact an organisation that supports managerial decision making or a strategic response.

2. Risk Framework
   The structure of an organisation that takes into consideration the expertise and capabilities, policies and procedures, and systems and controls that identify and mitigate procurement fraud risk.

3. Risk Strategy
   A published long-term approach that outlines which aspects of procurement fraud and its mitigation an organisation is developing.

CULTURE

Communication and engagement with staff, suppliers, partners and stakeholders are essential in building and sharing values and beliefs to protect revenues and ensure procurement outcomes are met. The flow of information within an organisation is assessed to help enhance its counter-fraud culture. Although there are many areas that should be considered, where fraud is suspected or identified, internal and external communication might include briefing on current or new typologies to staff and suppliers, introducing identified risks into the current training programmes and whether information should be updated within the central library to ensure that staff are kept up to date.

RISK REPORTING

The size, structure and international reach of an organisation is likely to affect the counter-fraud approach and internal reporting processes for an organisation's leadership to consider and manage risks.

1. Risk Committee
   Responsible for recording and updating the risk register and advising the board on current and future risk tolerance/appetite and mitigation strategy, and to oversee the implementation of the strategy.

2. Executive and Board
   Dependent on an organisation's structure, the risk committee can either report new risks to the executive or board, or it can be part of the designated compliance group's responsibility.

COMPLIANCE STRUCTURES

The primary role in the introduction of policies and procedures is to assist the efficiency and effectiveness in managing an organisation's outputs. However, when used alongside a compliance programme, it can assist in the identification and mitigation of risk.

1. Policies and procedures that include finance, procurement, asset management, security, quality assurance and recruitment can be used as fraud prevention tools and can also help identify procurement fraud risk where non-compliance is identified.
2. Policies and procedures that can be used to help identify internal corruption and fraud risk might include gifts and hospitality, expenses, conflicts of interest and codes of conduct, where non-compliance may be an indicator of corruption or fraud risk.

Having conducted an initial assessment of the procurement life cycle and an organisation's policies and procedures, expertise and capability, and systems and controls—and documenting what is currently in place to mitigate procurement fraud and corruption risk—we begin to create an outline of the gaps in our anti-corruption approach.

The illustration below sets out an example of information that should be documented and prioritised, along with recommended actions to mitigate current risk.

Risk Area	Typology	Risk	Priority	Improvement Opportunity/Proposed Mitigation
1. Fraud Prevention	Procurement Fraud	Lack of communication of strategy to staff, partners, suppliers and consultants		• Introduce a communication strategy to reinforce the organisation's stance on fraud and corruption and develop and enhance an counter-fraud and corruption culture
2. Fraud Risk Assessment	Procurement Fraud	Unable to assess the level of fraud risk that the organisation faces		• Create a centralised capability that collects and analyses all risk data to standardise the case management process and create an annual risk profile of fraud and corruption risk
3. Security	Corruption Bid Manipulation	A leak of internal information to a supplier to facilitate the illicit award of a contract		• Review of physical and IT security procedures to assess the level of insider and external threat
4. Security	Corruption	Supplier has unrestricted access to the procurement department		• Restricted access of non-procurement staff to the procurement department • Procurement meetings with suppliers should be documented and held in separate meeting rooms
5. Project Risk	Procurement Fraud	No assessment of fraud risk within projects, so unable to assess fraud loss		• Introduce a fraud and corruption risk assessment at the project-planning stage • Introduce a field compliance team to respond to identified risks within projects
6. Supplier Vetting	Conflicts of Interest	Lack of conflict-of-interest verification		• Standardised vendor checks to confirm whether there are conflicts of interest • Annual declaration of conflicts of interest by staff
7. Project Failures	Corruption Product Substitution	Lack of verification of supplier's ability to perform a contract		• Supplier visits during the vetting process to confirm expertise and capability • Supplier to verify previous works
8. Non-catalogue Spend	Fraud and Corruption	Unable to confirm whether non-catalogue spend is overused		• Audit of non-catalogue spend to ensure that organisational procedure (cost plus percentage) is complied with
9. Gifts and Hospitality	Bribery	Risk of misuse within gifts and hospitality		• Review of gift and hospitality procedures, including documented receipt and retention of information
10. Staff Employment	Corruption	Staff in key positions going to work for a supplier		• Introduce an exit risk assessment procedure when key staff go to work for an organisation's supplier

CHAPTER 5
Typologies of Procurement Fraud and Corruption

The typologies of procurement fraud and corruption are diverse in nature, and it is only through understanding the various methods of each typology and where they can be used in targeting a procurement or project lifecycle—and by whom—can you more accurately assess these risks and introduce adequate mitigation.

The losses highlighted within the Introduction point out some of the common typologies used globally and the financial impact they can have. It is not uncommon for functions that directly or indirectly deal with procurement, which include finance, quality assurance, asset management, project management or other areas of the supply chain, including compliance, to have limited or no awareness of the breadth of procurement fraud and how and where it can impact an organisation.

Defining procurement fraud

There is no one definition of procurement fraud. However, to acquire a greater understanding of the scale and diversity of the risk, and identify where your organisation, procurement process or projects can be targeted, it has been separated into the components of procurement and fraud.

DEFINING PROCUREMENT

The procurement process can cover the acquisition of goods, works or services—including both the acquisition from third parties and in-house providers—and spans the whole life cycle, from the identification of needs through to the end of a contract or the end of the useful life and disposal of an asset.

DEFINING FRAUD

Given the varying international legislative definitions of fraud, it is simpler to note that fraud that impacts the procurement process can be described as a fraudulent act committed against an organisation's procurement process. In looking at the elements of fraud[6] from the UK Fraud Act 2006, within procurement the dishonest act can be divided into three parts:

1. Making **a false representation** and intending, by making the representation, to make a gain for himself or another, or to cause loss to another or expose another to a risk of loss.
2. An **abuse of position**, which occurs where a person who occupies a position in which he is expected to safeguard, or not to act against, the financial interest of another person dishonestly abuses that position and intends, by means of the abuse of that position, to make a gain for himself or another or to cause loss to another or to expose another to a risk of loss.
3. **Failing to disclose** to another person information which he is under a legal duty to disclose and intends, by failing to disclose the information, to make a gain for himself or another or to cause loss to another or to expose another to a risk of loss.

---

[6] https://www.legislation.gov.uk/ukpga/2006/35/section/1

Procurement fraud typologies

There are a significant number of procurement fraud typologies that can on occasion create a risk that is unknown or misunderstood. The main typologies are described below, but within each typology there can be many methods with which each typology can be committed.

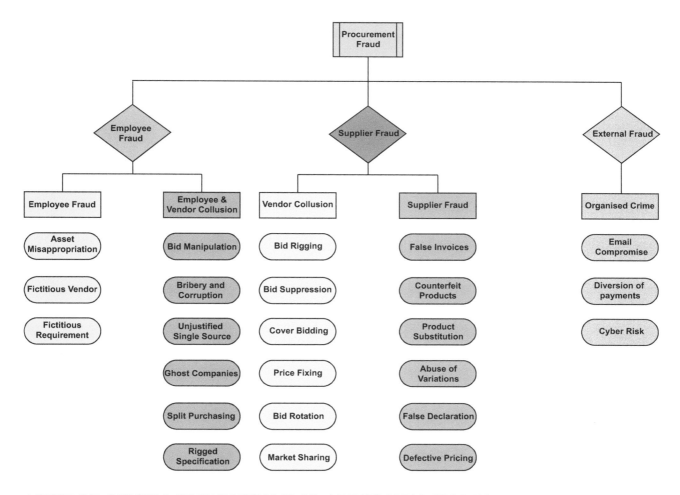

ABUSE OF CONTRACT VARIATIONS OR ADDITIONAL WORKS

Contract variations or a submission of additional-works requests can be manipulated or falsified. Where additional works/variations are requested, this can render the project susceptible to fraud, unless the correct monitoring, auditing and authorisation processes are in place.

ASSET MISAPPROPRIATION

This refers to the theft of procured assets, which can include by the manipulation or falsification of an organisation's controls, documentation or movement or disposal of materials.

BID MANIPULATION

An insider can manipulate the bidding process in many ways to benefit a favoured contractor or supplier, eliminating the competition within the bidding process. Examples can include accepting late bids, leaking information and rebidding for the agreed vendor to enhance their bid. Additionally, inviting poor or inadequate suppliers to submit bids will allow a favoured supplier to win a contract. This corruption could be conducted to support a cartel, including where the bid evaluation process is being manipulated (i.e. information is left out or the insider is used to rig the bids, where a new competitors bid is submitted, that are not part of the cartel).

BID RIGGING

Bid rigging involves companies colluding together to influence a competitive bidding process and secure a predetermined contract award and price.

BID ROTATION

In this scheme, all competitors collude to submit bids but take turns at being the lowest bidder. Competitors who are part of the cartel can take turns on the winning bid or being the agreed subcontractor, depending on the size and value of the contract.

BID SUPPRESSION

One or more competitors who would have been expected to bid agree to refrain from bidding or to withdraw a previously submitted bid so that an agreed colluding competitor's bid is accepted.

BRIBERY AND CORRUPTION

Bribery involves an offer, promise or payment of a bribe, and corruption includes the request, receipt or agreeing to receive a pecuniary advantage to influence the procurement process—including the award of a contract—allowing illicit overcharging, false invoicing, product substitution or acceptance of substandard goods, materials, works or services within the contract. The payment or pecuniary advantage can be anything of value.

CARTELS

A cartel is a collection of companies that act together to influence price and the market for certain goods, works and services by controlling production and marketing.

COMPLEMENTARY (COVER) BIDDING

This bid rigging method is conducted when competitors agree to submit either complementary high bids or a bid with additional terms that they know will not be accepted. These activities give the appearance of competition and are the most common forms of bid rigging schemes. This allows their preselected contractor to win contracts, either on a rotating basis or with the winning contractor sharing the profits between parties.

COUNTERFEIT PRODUCTS

All aspects of the fraudulent product and package are fully replicated, and the product or raw materials can be substandard, unregistered or unlicensed, or falsely represent their identity, composition or source.

CYBER-THREAT

In addition to areas such as email compromise, there exists online procurement fraud threat from fake or copied websites, where goods purchased will either not be provided or are inferior, substituted or counterfeit.

DEFECTIVE PRICING

The deliberate use of inaccurate cost or pricing information to inflate costs and the total value of a contract.

DIVERSION OF PAYMENTS

During an ongoing procurement contract or project, an insider requests or changes a supplier's bank account details to divert payments to a personal bank account, or illicitly changes a supplier's bank account details by creating a false letter of request from the supplier to change payment information. Additionally, through a similar process, where there is unauthorised access to a supplier's information—or through cyber-crime and business email compromise, using the compromised email—clients are requested to change current payment information to a new bank account to divert current or future payments to a new account controlled by criminals.

EMAIL COMPROMISE

In situations where an organisation's email system is targeted, either by creating an email address that is similar to a known email address—usually with a one-character difference in the address—or where their email system is compromised or hacked, this opportunity is used to contact an organisation's clients to inform them of a change of bank account details and that future invoices are to be paid into the new account.

FALSE DECLARATIONS

Information that can be provided during pre-and post-contract award stages that enables fraud to occur (e.g. the provision of false, out-of-date or inflated pricing information within the negotiation process, which allows higher invoicing within the contract).

FALSE INVOICING

This involves the submission of invoices for works, services or goods that were not or were only partially provided. There are many examples of false invoicing, including duplicate billing, claims made for additional workers who were not present (ghost workers) or abuse of time cards. The costs have not occurred, are not reasonable or cannot be directly or indirectly allocated to the contract.

FICTITIOUS VENDORS

Fictitious vendors are placed on the supplier list and false invoices are created and used to either divert illicit payments to others or facilitate the theft of monies from the organisation.

GHOST/SHELL COMPANIES

Ghost/shell companies can be set up and used to bid for tenders and, where contracts are won, monies can be asked for upfront before any goods, works or services are provided. The goods, works or services will either not be provided or will be only partially supplied. A company may set up the business with a name that is the same as or similar to a well-known brand or create a website to support the appearance of legitimacy of a ghost/shell company.

INFLATED CLAIMS AND MISCHARGING

Practices relating to the submission of false invoices that involve billing for higher costs for goods, works or services provided, including through the increase in the quantity of materials used or services provided, or increasing the number of staff or hourly/daily rate.

MARKET SHARING

Market sharing involves companies dividing markets or product lines and agreeing not to compete against each other. This can occur where products or services are specialist and very few companies regionally, nationally or globally are involved in the product manufacture or provision of the goods or services.

PRICE FIXING

Once a bid rigging scheme is in place, it can fix the contracting price by increasing the value of the lowest bid, thereby creating greater profit to share between colluding companies. It can additionally be linked to market sharing, where companies that control the market decide to fix prices at an agreed rate.

PRODUCT SUBSTITUTION

A contractor or vendor substitutes products with material of lesser quality than specified or uses counterfeit, defective, substandard, falsified, or used parts or products.

PURCHASES FOR PERSONAL USE OR RESALE

An insider uses a purchase system to procure items that they intended for their own use, resale or, as part of an organised crime. Goods are identified and stolen to order, and several individuals might be involved in the acquisition and transportation of the stolen goods. The purchase information can be altered, falsified, or destroyed to hide the originator/creator of the paperwork.

RIGGED DESIGN OR SPECIFICATION

An insider or consulting company unduly manipulates the design or specification of an organisation's requirement to influence the award of a contract or allow a favoured contractor to qualify for a bidding process for which they would not otherwise have qualified. A rigged design or specification may also be used to create contract variations later on in a project, where design flaws or additional works are identified.

SPLIT PURCHASING

Procurement is deliberately split into two or more purchases so that each purchase is below the financial threshold that would otherwise have required additional financial scrutiny or a competitive tender process.

UNJUSTIFIED SINGLE/SOLE SOURCE

This involves an insider deliberately writing a non-supportable single source justification or using this procurement route to avoid a competitive tender selection, and illicitly or improperly awarding a contract to a predetermined vendor.

Scope of procurement fraud

Although the typologies of procurement fraud will be discussed in more detail, when the scope of procurement fraud is considered, there are four areas that need to be examined:

1. The insider fraud, where an individual or individuals steal an organisation's assets or monies and, on many occasions, create a false requirement, false documentation or a fictitious vendor to facilitate or hide the illicit activity.
2. External fraud committed by a single supplier where, for example, false invoices are submitted for services that were not provided or a group of companies collude together during the bidding process to inflate prices or manipulate the award of a contract to an agreed company.

3. Fraud and corruption where a member of staff or other insider colludes with a vendor or supplier to manipulate or influence the procurement life cycle, including the prior- or post-award process, which could include the falsification of quality, quantities, resources, time and cost within contract management.

4. Individual criminal activity or enterprise that targets an organisation's procurement or financial system to illicitly divert payments or procurement through fraud or false representation by way of illicit email compromise or other communication imitating a supplier and requesting a change of bank account details to divert supplier invoice payments.

Elements of procurement fraud

Several countries have attempted to define procurement fraud within national legislation. To define procurement fraud and its extent the elements of the UK fraud definition has been used, to include fraud by false representation, abuse of position and failure to disclose information. In using this approach, the various typologies of procurement fraud can be more simply categorised.

False representation

When we consider the various methods of fraud by **false representation** within procurement, some examples of fraud indicators might include:

1. creating a false statement of requirement for vehicle rental that is then used for personal use
2. introducing a fictitious vendor on an organisation's procurement system to give the appearance of competition when used within tenders, or used to illicitly divert payments where a fictitious requirement is created
3. providing inflated scoring as part of the tender board to assist a vendor to win a contract
4. knowingly misrepresenting counterfeit parts from a supplier as the original manufacturer
5. assisting invoicing or bonus payments to a contractor and approving completion certificates for payment when work is ongoing or has not commenced
6. obtaining a contract by providing false information on a company's ability to perform work
7. submission of a falsified letter to change a supplier's bank account details to illicitly divert payments to an account set up to launder the stolen payments
8. within a chemical and remediation contract, the contractor improperly and illicitly disposing of chemicals in landfill or national water systems

Abuse of position

When examining the various methods of fraud by **abuse of position,** some of the examples of fraud indicators might include:

1. misuse of blanket purchase orders for non-catalogue purchases to inflate prices to hide a kickback
2. invoices being authorised without a purchase order or requisition
3. using role and position to override organisational processes and controls
4. manipulating financial data, which may include duplicate entries, change of bank details and diverting payments to other accounts

5. inputting incomplete data into a procurement system to hide collusion and fraud by the supplier
6. misuse of rental contracts, where there is limited oversight of this type of procurement or management of assets
7. misuse of procurement cards for personal purchases
8. splitting orders to avoid the additional oversight and the need to introduce the tender process
9. the purchase of goods above the market price to benefit suppliers with whom they have a conflict-of-interest business relationship or to receive a kickback from the purchase
10. illicit repeat purchasing of low-quality goods from the same supplier

Failure to disclose information

When we examine the various methods of fraud by **failure to disclose** information, some of the examples of these fraud indicators would include:

1. an individual deliberately failing to disclose a conflict of interest when requested to do so as part of an organisation's compliance procedures and later using their position to divert contracts to the company
2. a manager withholding their shareholding with an organisation's supplier when involved in the tender selection process
3. a staff member going to work for a supplier shortly after their involvement in the contract award
4. a supplier knowingly receiving counterfeit parts from their supply chain and using them within a client solution
5. during the registration process, where required to do so, a vendor deliberately failing to disclose the details of a board member who is a PEP
6. a supplier obtaining a contract by not providing information on their inability to perform work, which might include financial standing

PRE-CONTRACT AWARD RISK

To recognise where the procurement process can be targeted by fraud and corruption, including the typologies that can be used, the key stages of the procurement process must first be set out and assessed for risk.

Up to the point of contract award, there are many areas of the process in which individuals who are involved in the decision making can influence or manipulate the process to facilitate fraud.

CORRUPTION RISKMAP

NEED
Define business need and create business case

DESIGN
Develop design and specification

ANALYSIS
Market analysis and make or buy decision

ROUTE
Agree on procurement method

SELECT
Supplier selection for single source or restricted tender process

TENDER
Bid evaluation and scoring

AWARD
Contract award and implementation

CONTRACT
Contract management

PERFORM
Contract performance and suppler engagement

ASSETS
Asset management and disposal

The insider threats and risks within these key areas might include the following:

1. Within the initial **identification of need**—where there is no clear decision making, management or oversight of this stage—there may be an opportunity for a requirement to be invented, falsified or overstated to influence the contract award or divert procurement or project funds during contract management.
2. Where **market analysis** is not carried out or a contract is awarded far in excess of the market price for goods or services.
3. Fraud risk can be created within procurement where there is a lack of **justification** or clear evidence within a **business case** or where there is an overemphasis of the business benefit to justify the inflated funding required.
4. Where the **design stage** of a project or asset is used to favour a specific vendor or where a design is deliberately inadequate so that it will require additional variations within a project or at contract management stage. This will enable a vendor to submit a low bid in the knowledge that they will recover these losses through the lifetime of the contract.

5. The **scope and specification** of a requirement can be manipulated in several ways, including being used to introduce additional requirements into a project or contract that aren't necessary or being written to favour a specific vendor or designate a brand product when a generic brand product would suffice.

6. A **budget** or cost estimate is falsified or inflated to incorporate the bribe payment or a level of fraud, or within projects where more than one cost centre or budget is used to hide the total cost of a project. Budget variances may be an indicator that initial estimates may have been deliberately kept low to give the appearance of value for money.

7. Deliberate analysis of price information that does not include **total cost analysis** may assist a vendor bidding low to win a tender and recovering losses after the award through contract variations or ongoing service requirements such as facilities management.

8. Where **financial thresholds** are introduced to ensure that there is additional oversight in the authorisation process or change in the procurement route, these thresholds can be manipulated in several ways, including split purchasing to keep procurement under these financial limits.

9. The **procurement route** can be manipulated away from the tender process to single source procurement or a restricted tender to avoid or limit competition, ensuring that a designated vendor is awarded the contract.

10. Particularly within restricted tenders or low-value procurement to manipulate the tender process, **vendor identification** is used to give the appearance of competition, where vendors who will not pass the evaluation process are identified and ensured that the agreed vendor will receive that contract award.

11. Low-value procurement procedures, where **three quotes** are required for best-value selection—either creating fictitious quotes or deliberately obtaining high-value quotes to ensure the award—is given to a pre-agreed vendor. Fraud and corruption indicators might include the same vendor being used or winning this type of procurement and the total value of these purchases being significant, or the goods or services not being part of a vendor's business.

12. The **pre-qualification** process can be manipulated where poorly written or false vendor submissions are deliberately allowed through this process.

13. The bidding process can be manipulated in several ways, including during the **bid response,** where timescales are short, ensuring that minimal responses are received within the competitive process so that a vendor who has received prior notice is awarded the contract. Analysing patterns in the tender process in the areas discussed would also include the percentage and the root cause of bids where only one vendor responded.

14. The **scoring matrix** can be used to manipulate vendor selection through the introduction of a new scoring matrix or the amendment or addition of selection criteria to manipulate supplier selection.

15. **Vendor selection** during the tender process can be manipulated through a conflict of interest and deliberate inaccurate or inflated scoring.

16. Through delays to the **selection process** or repeating the selection process to ensure that the prior agreed vendor is awarded the contract. Instances where a company declines the award may indicate bid rigging between the vendors.

Scope of work and specification

The scope of work and specification areas of the pre-tender phase can hide many opportunities for fraud or the design of fraud into the contract and its management. There can be several internal or external stakeholders involved in the development of a specification—including product designers or engineers, end-users, procurement or brand expertise—and this involvement may be used to influence the product design, development and specification, which may ultimately be used to manipulate the tender and award of a contract. These actions might include:

1. creating a technical specification or specifying bespoke items to fit the products or capabilities of a particular contractor or creating a narrow specification that limits the supplier base to manipulate the selection
2. over-specification, which reduces the number of competitive bidders that have such a product or would have increased costs in the design and creation of this requirement
3. creating a specification that is so restrictive or vague that potential firms that would normally compete do not submit bids or are unable to provide accurate commercial bid submissions
4. deliberate under-specification that will lead to variations within the contract term and increased billing by the contractor
5. using a statement of work, specifications or sole source justification developed by, or in consultation with, a preferred contractor
6. improper release of information by firms participating in project design to contractors competing for the prime contract
7. designing pre-qualification standards or specifications to exclude otherwise qualified contractors or their products or to include contractors who would normally have been excluded at this stage
8. the vendor not having the required technical expertise, so would otherwise be excluded during tender assessment
9. splitting up requirements so that contractors each get a 'fair share' and can rotate bids, a mix of bid manipulation and bid rigging
10. bid specifications or statements of work not being consistent with items included in general requirements
11. specifications that are not consistent with previous procurement or similar projects

Procurement route

Tender process

The bidding process and tender selection is recognised as one of the high-risk areas within the procurement process, where bribery and corruption can influence or manipulate decision making and contract award. Examples of such risk might include:

1. split purchasing to avoid the tender process
2. use of short timescales for bid returns to manipulate the number of bid submissions
3. inflating technical scoring as part of the tender selection to assist a vendor to win the contract
4. improper justification for single source procurement to avoid a competitive tender selection and illicitly award a contract to a predetermined vendor
5. failing to disclose personal or business relationship during the tender selection process
6. leaks of commercial information, including competitors' technical or pricing information to a competing vendor
7. improper vendor identification being used to give the appearance of competition during a restricted tender, where vendors who have inferior products or services, and will not pass the evaluation process, are identified
8. advanced notice or selective release, by employees, of information concerning requirements and pending purchases to 'preferred' contractors to influence the tender process
9. the use of unqualified bidders in restricted tender, including companies where the category of goods or services required is not part of a vendor's business
10. a call for tender not being published in official journals or being limited to a website that isn't viewed regularly, reducing the opportunity for legitimate companies to compete
11. a tender being extended after the closing date to share commercial and technical information received from bidding companies

12. tender submissions or communications outside the published channels
13. in countries where local content is an advantage within the tender process and where there are limited national companies that provide the same or similar quality of service that international companies provide, the tender scoring or selection is manipulated to corruptly award a contract to a company that has inferior goods, works or services

Contract award

Tender selection and contract award are recognised as one of the high-risk areas within procurement, where bribery and corruption can influence decision making. Indicators that may highlight that there is a problem in these areas might include:

1. the contract award is being given to a vendor with a known history of poor performance
2. the contract award is being given to a contractor who is neither the lowest price nor the most technically qualified
3. the winning bidder declining the contract award and suggesting that a competing vendor is awarded the contract
4. disqualification of a bidder without justification, and a lack of tender documentation and communication to manipulate the contract award and hide the illicit behaviour
5. contract variation or a change to an order shortly after the contract is awarded
6. bribery to affect the terms or schedule of rates of a contract
7. advanced payments being agreed without justification and against procurement policy
8. a large percentage of contracts being awarded to one vendor, or a vendor consistently winning bids when there are superior bid submissions

In 2015 a piece of research was published by the European Commission[7] outlining the number of bid responses received for UK Government contracts between 2009 and 2013. In 3.38% of cases only one returning bid was received and in 5.12% of cases only two bid responses were received, a total of 8.5% of bids between the two: a total of 9,231.

The research does not consider the root cause of why there is such a low return rate of bid submissions or the type of contract being tendered. However, when we take into account the risk of insider influence on the procurement process and external bid rigging schemes to influence the award of contracts, if there is not already the risk of procurement fraud, it creates an opportunity for fraud and corruption to be introduced.

Single source procurement

Unjustified single source procurement can be used inappropriately to avoid the tender process or directly award a contract to a vendor by corrupt means. Examples and indicators of this type of fraud and corruption might include:

1. an inaccurate or poorly written justification for single source procurement
2. no single source justification form completed or authorised
3. improper use of security or national security shroud to amend the procurement route
4. commonly available services that have not been single sourced previously

---

[7] Source: own calculations using European Commission-DG Internal Market and Services (2015)

5. a significant percentage of purchases of non-catalogue on high-value items at cost plus 10% where a lower cost plus percentage would have been expected
6. the supplier not being registered for a category of work or services, or the supplier not having carried out this type of work before
7. improper use of an urgent requirement to justify single source procurement
8. using consultants who are known to, or are a friend of, the end-user or the person justifying the requirement

Auctions

In circumstances where an organisation uses auctions or online auction sites to sell its goods, or uses the opportunity to dispose of organisational materials that would otherwise be scrapped, there are occasions where fraud risk might present itself.

1. A false representation of the quality or authenticity of the goods and price.
2. A false representation of the value of the goods to facilitate their purchase by an agreed buyer at a low or minimal cost.
3. Manipulation of the auction environment might include the marketing of the event or misrepresenting items to be sold to reduce the number of bidders and end-value.
4. Auctioneer misrepresentation of services and performance.
5. Use of fake bidders to inflate competing bids.

Reverse auctions

A reverse auction can be described as a type of auction in which the normal roles of buyer and seller are reversed. In a reverse auction the sellers compete to obtain business from the buyer, and prices will typically decrease as the sellers underbid each other. To gain a commercial advantage, there may be occasions where the process is improperly manipulated:

1. Where the purpose of procurement is to obtain the lowest price, driving a price down may push a vendor to introduce inferior, substituted or counterfeit products.
2. Where there are a limited number of bidding vendors, it may create a bid rigging environment where suppliers agree to high prices and rotate winning bidders.
3. Use of fake bids or buyers to decrease the value of the reverse bid.

Purchasing cards

Procurement cards can be a valuable tool in the enhancement of an organisation's purchasing efficiency and cost reduction. However, where there is a weak policy or a limited compliance programme, there may be a significant risk of fraud and theft within this purchase route. The illicit misuse of purchasing cards may be for personal use or as part of a fraud scheme, where common illicit purchasing methods might include:

1. amending a delivery address to a personal address or the address of an individual who is part of a fraud scheme
2. not adding a procured item on an organisation's asset register and stealing the item once the goods have been received
3. paying a supplier as part of a fraud scheme where the goods were not provided
4. purchasing goods outside the scope of procurement policy
5. duplicating purchases, where an individual uses a procurement card to pay for expenses and then claims for the expense separately

E-procurement systems

There can be significant fraud risk within an organisation's electronic procurement system, where proper controls, audit and data management are not in place. Examples of such risk might include:

1. where bid submissions are not securely held and can be opened by the end-user before the closing date, allowing individuals to share information with a competing bidder
2. where extensions are made after the bidding closing date, allowing the end-user to share pricing and technical information about the current bidders with a new competitor
3. where the scope of the procurement is poorly defined, which means companies are unable to properly provide accurate pricing information, apart from a company that has received insider information of budgets or additional technical information that was not shared with other bidders
4. the common method of introducing short timescales for bid responses, which are used to ensure that minimal replies are received, and a colluding bidder receiving early notice of the requirement
5. where contact details are given on a tender advertisement and where a poorly defined scope is published, forcing vendors to make contact to request additional information—this creates an opportunity for the individual receiving the request for additional information to request a bribe and an opportunity to manipulate the bid toward the bribe payer
6. an opportunity and commercial advantage, during the bidding process, for vendors to clarify information around the procurement requirement that is not shared with other vendors
7. missing procurement data from the system, including contract or company information—is it human error or is it a deliberate attempt to hide fraud?

Outsourcing

The outsourcing of internal business services—including the onboarding of vendors, payment, and procurement capabilities—can be perceived as an opportunity for cost efficiency and to reduce or outsource risk. However, when assessing organisational risk and liability within the extraterritorial reach of bribery and corruption legislation, such as the United Kingdom Bribery Act 2010 and the United States of America Foreign Corrupt Practices Act 1977 (FCPA), the risk, liability and potential impact are likely to remain with the organisation where there is a breach of law by the third party. In considering risk and mitigation when outsourcing is being assessed, several areas should be considered:

1. Security and confidentiality risks
2. Vetting of vendor executives and consultants
3. Expertise and solutions
4. Quality of services and ability to monitor and manage contract performance
5. Loss of control and oversight of the process

Procurement corruption

Insider threat

There are many areas and roles within an organisation where individuals can influence the procurement process. The challenge when having an insider threat is that it will likely be known where the control weaknesses are and how to circumvent them. As corruption is an illicit connection between individuals, it is at these touch points—where individuals connect with the supply chain, control measures and suppliers—that the risk increases.

Insider information

There are several roles and key points within the procurement life cycle where an individual can share information with a vendor to influence the award of a contract, including:

1. design and specification information to assist in the completion of a vendor's technical bid
2. budget and internal pricing information to assist a vendor to more accurately complete their commercial bid
3. sharing bidding companies' submissions with another vendor
4. sharing historical bid submissions to assist a vendor in future bids

Ghost companies

A ghost company is generally a company that has no assets or resources and has been set up to divert funds that have been obtained from procurement fraud, theft or corruption. The use of single source procurement is the simplest way to divert funds to ghost companies. Generally, these companies can be used in organisations that have weak vendor registration controls or where an employee can order, receive and approve payments for goods or services. Indicators might include:

1. payment to a vendor not on the approved vendor list
2. vendors not listed in business or telephone directories
3. invoiced goods or services that cannot be located or verified
4. a vendor's address being a Mail forwarding address or PO Box
5. the ghost company being used as a sub-contractor, where its details or ownership will not be checked by the client
6. the company being linked to an offshore account to hide the beneficial owner

Manipulation of specification

The specification can be manipulated or created around a supplier's product or services to influence a tender award, particularly where other contractors have the additional cost of manufacture instead of an off-the-shelf product. Indicators of this type of fraud might include:

1. fewer than normal bidders responding to the request for a proposal
2. the specification not being approved or signed off
3. the specification or scope being too narrow, so that it does not allow a vendor to accurately prepare a technical bid
4. a specification or scope being too broad, so that it does not assist a vendor to accurately prepare the commercial bid
5. specifying the use of a brand name when a generic brand could be used or has been used before
6. the specification of the winning vendor being the same or similar to the organisation's requirement

Bid manipulation

Bid manipulation can occur when an individual within the bidding process uses their position to influence an individual or the procurement process for the benefit of a vendor. Indicators of fraud risk in this area might include:

1. creating a short deadline for bid submissions, which does not allow time or gives limited time for competing companies to submit bids
2. deliberately not advertising the bid publicly

3. within restricted tenders, not inviting the current service provider to bid on the new tender
4. deliberately inviting poor-performing vendors to bid, giving the appearance of competition
5. quick vendor submissions to a complex requirement
6. late bids being allowed in the tender selection process after the closing date
7. improperly qualifying bidding companies or disqualifying strong bid submissions
8. few returns from vendors or fewer than available suppliers being asked to bid
9. vendor clarifications that are not shared with other bidding companies
10. immediate or quick mobilisation, which might indicate that the vendor had prior knowledge of a requirement or it had previously been agreed that they would win the contract
11. inappropriate contact with a vendor during the solicitation, evaluation or negotiation processes
12. the services not previously being provided by the vendor, or the vendor being unable or unqualified to provide the specification, and yet they are still awarded the contract
13. work commencing before a contractor is selected or a contract awarded
14. the unauthorised release of commercially sensitive information to a vendor to support their bid submission

Asset misappropriation

Procured assets can be misappropriated through theft or fraud that can be hidden by the creation of false or forged documentation and is recognised as a significant financial risk by many global organisations. Asset misappropriation can be exhibited in many forms to facilitate the theft, including assets and their status being misdescribed. Such examples include:

1. documenting new or good-quality assets as lost, scrap, damaged or obsolete
2. assets being written-off when their location cannot be identified
3. the deliberate undervalue of assets to sell to an agreed vendor during disposal procedures
4. overstating materials required or creating a fictitious requirement to facilitate procurement where items will be illicitly removed later

Where a significant loss or missing assets are identified and documented as part of an audit, individuals in many cases don't consider that these items have been stolen. Where investigation or additional risk mitigation isn't introduced into the asset management process, it is likely that these thefts will continue.

Organisational assets

What is regarded as an asset can vary between organisations but may include cash, information, machinery, inventory, non-inventory items, land, buildings and copyright or trademark. Inventory management and the replenishment of high-volume items in areas such as maintenance, repair and operating supplies can create a significant procurement fraud risk and financial loss where there is a limited or lack of:

1. procurement monitoring and goods receipts, including receipt, inspection and acceptance
2. asset tracking, including receipt, issue and transfer of materials
3. stock integrity—including obsolescence, damage, deterioration or loss—assessing the level of risk or identified patterns that might include the increase in stock purchases or disposal
4. oversight or available information where purchases are directed towards a current or a new supplier for items on a single source basis
5. the ability to audit an inventory management system

Insider threat in asset management

An environment and opportunity for fraud may be created where there is limited or a lack of asset management and tracking or where there is limited expertise within warehouse management or compliance programmes. Indicators of theft or fraud risk might include:

1. regular losses of high-value, repeat or attractive items, such as computers
2. materials overstated within projects
3. improper justification for overstocking
4. missing or incomplete data within goods receipts, asset register, requisition, purchase orders or invoices
5. high levels of write-offs, scrap, and damaged or obsolescent equipment
6. significant losses of equipment in transit
7. poor tracking of assets where there are significant losses
8. a lack of information or unusual routes for the disposal of assets

RENTAL

As part of the financial management within an organisation, or as part of a contractor's project requirement, rental of equipment or vehicles is common for its financial efficiency. However, if proper asset management is not in place, fraud may be introduced into rental contracts in the following ways:

1. Creating a false statement of requirement of vehicle rental that is then used for personal use—this can be particularly relevant where projects are spread over large distances and no one has the responsibility of verifying its usage
2. Evidence of deliberate delays in a project to incur an additional cost, including rental of equipment
3. Equipment being charged more than the rental period
4. The misuse of rental rates or quantity of vehicles or equipment as laid out within contract terms
5. Rentals used on other projects and double billed
6. The submission of false invoices and supporting paperwork for rental of vehicles when personal vehicles are used

External threat in asset management

An external threat, which may include a fraud scheme involving an insider, may present itself in several ways:

1. Payment for incomplete orders
2. Overbilling or over-ordering of the same goods from the same supplier
3. An outside business interest in individuals working within the procurement life cycle, including undisclosed conflicts of interest
4. Refurbishment of equipment by a vendor and resale as new
5. Creation of false records, including delivery and movement records

Corrupt practices

The Department of Justice (DOJ) and the Securities and Exchange Commission (SEC) in the United States of America—in the resolution of Foreign Corrupt Practices Act (FCPA) 1977 actions—annually publish their financial punishments and recoveries. During 2020 they recovered $2.2 billion in total fines, penalties and disgorgement imposed in corporate settlements. In the main, the common types of bribery and corruption methods within these FCPA cases include:

1. payment of cash
2. gifts, travel, tickets, hospitality, meals and entertainment
3. shares
4. employment to relatives, friends and associates of government officials
5. donations to foreign government agencies
6. electronic payment via a third party or offshore company

In their aim to hide the illicit nature of covert relations with the government official or PEPs, including the bribery purpose and payments, the bribery routes taken were varied. They included:

1. storage contracts with a company owned by the son of the government official—no items were ever stored
2. sham consultancy agreements
3. the use of third parties, agents and intermediaries to make payments
4. the use of discounts to fund improper payments
5. the use of off-book slush funds
6. the use of offshore companies and bank accounts, which continues to be a common method of hiding the bribe payment, including the government official having a financial interest in or beneficial ownership of the offshore company
7. the use of service providers

The use of consultants or sham consultancy contracts as a method of false billing and bribery or to hide the illicit payment appears to be the most common method of bribery. To hide the bribery, several methods were used to conceal these payments and falsify records. These included:

1. the destruction of records
2. falsified contract changes to orders to hide the bribe payment
3. the use of fake invoices to conceal bribery and create slush funds
4. the creation of consultancy firm due diligence reports that missed out family links to a government office
5. commissioning payments to third parties, agents or intermediaries

In addition to the bribery methods already mentioned, there are many other ways in which a bribe can be paid that does not include direct cash payments:

1. Sponsorship for personal or other private activities
2. Construction or other services provided at a home address or other location
3. Excessive gifts and hospitality
4. Company shares and dividend payments
5. Company employment of family members
6. Acquisition of property or other items of high value
7. Charity or political donations

How are contract funds diverted or laundered?

Where corruption is used to commit fraud within procurement or to divert assets, some of the common methods in which funds and criminal proceeds can be diverted or laundered include:

1. the use of a sub-contractor to facilitate the bribery payments that are linked to the corrupt individuals who helped facilitate the contract award or other procurement fraud
2. the creation of a fictitious sub-contractor to facilitate the bribe payment to the corrupt individual(s)
3. the use of consultancy contracts or fictitious consultancy contracts to divert funds to a corrupt insider, where payments are made for services that aren't provided
4. manipulation of a vendor's payment details on an organisation's financial system, which may include a change of bank account information submitted to the finance department to illicitly divert funds
5. where an organisation has poor vendor onboarding in place, ghost companies being used with offshore bank accounts to divert payments when no works or services are provided or are provided but are of poor or substandard quality

Procurement corruption and associated money laundering

Due to the covert nature of procurement fraud and corruption, in many cases bribe payments, diverted funds and payment from the contract fraud can be difficult to trace, as can the identity of the person(s) who received the funds. This can be particularly challenging where records are not created or are destroyed to hide the illicit conduct. In addition to the banking sector, there are many routes individuals can take to hide the proceeds of their crime:

1. the real estate and hospitality industry
2. trade-based money laundering
3. undeclared funds moved across borders
4. use of legitimate and front companies to conceal beneficial owners and move funds
5. former government employees setting up companies that were used to receive funds from the government
6. securities or insurances
7. motor vehicles
8. education and payment of fees
9. smuggling of cash, including the use of money transfer businesses
10. use of offshore bank accounts in foreign jurisdictions
11. casinos

External threats

The external procurement fraud threat can be significant and varied, and when supported by an insider, can not only have a greater impact but can also facilitate fraud and corruption from being detected.

DEFECTIVE PRICING

In instances where companies look to maximise profits during a contract by deliberately introducing inflated pricing compared to normal costs, and this information isn't known to or verified by the procuring organisation, this ultimately increases the contract value:

1. where costs or pricing have decreased and vendor fails to pass on reductions, which might include deliberately not passing on discounts
2. where the contractor uses out-of-date pricing schedules within commercial proposal
3. where different materials to those listed within a contract are used
4. where contractors are using under-qualified personnel or subcontractors and are charging for increased levels of expertise within the schedule of rates

5. where false or deliberately altered costs and calculations are created to support a proposal submission

OVERCHARGING

It is not uncommon for vendors to provide a low price to ensure that they win a competitive tender and then try to recover these monies through fraud or other illicit activity during the lifetime of the contract. Common methods of overcharging are through time, quality, quantity, price and resources. Indicators of overcharging might include:

1. invoicing for increased headcount, more than is present, or providing a reduced headcount than that required within the contract but invoicing for contracted numbers
2. billing for inflated hours for contractors or equipment used on a project
3. billing for the same resources on multiple projects
4. billing for a higher specification of materials than those provided
5. no supporting paperwork for invoices
6. prices not matching the schedule of rates or blanket purchase agreements
7. vague line descriptions, including a variety of rates, that prevents accurate verification
8. billing for the cost of a senior consultant and substituting lower-skilled or less-qualified employees or consultants to undertake the work

FALSE CLAIMS

False claims can include the submission of false or inflated invoices for goods, works or services that were not provided or were already paid for, or values and quantities inflated or misrepresented. Examples of fraud indicators might include:

1. an invoice that is received in a different format than usual from a supplier
2. no evidence that the goods, works or services were carried out or received
3. the invoice not matching the requisition or purchase order
4. billing for working hours increased without evidence or justification
5. no goods receipt note or the asset not being recorded within the organisation's asset register
6. invoicing for work that has already been billed for
7. the same invoice values for different goods, works or services provided by the same supplier, which may indicate a fictitious requirement
8. invoice numbers being in consecutive order

COUNTERFEIT PRODUCTS

Counterfeit, inferior or substituted products can impact all sectors where there is profit to be made from these goods, particularly from items that can be produced in volume to maximise profits. The variations of these products might include:

1. a component of a legitimate product that is fraudulent
2. a fake product designed to look like and exact copy of the legitimate product
3. all aspects of the fraudulent product and packaging being fully replicated
4. the World Health Organisation (WHO), when defining counterfeit pharmaceuticals, categorising them as 'substandard, unregistered or unlicensed and falsified medical products'

Although the retail sector is the main sector impacted, there are several sectors where health and safety and threat to life are at significant risk from counterfeiting, including medical equipment and pharmaceuticals, vehicle and aircraft parts, electronics, chemicals and pesticides. Having a reporting system to record equipment failure and maintenance regimes can be an important part of risk assessment and testing for counterfeits.

DIVERSION OF PAYMENTS

Illicitly changing supplier bank account details and diverting payments into accounts controlled by criminals can be carried out in several ways.

1. A letter purporting to be from a supplier, received by the finance or procurement department, requesting that future payments are made to the new bank account details enclosed within the letter.
2. An insider with unauthorised access to supplier or contract information, including administration access where authority has not been removed when an individual moves within an organisation or leaves the organisation.
3. Cyber-crime and business email compromise, where a client is contacted from a perceived trusted email account, or similar account, to divert current or future payments intended for a supplier to an account controlled by criminals.

BUSINESS EMAIL COMPROMISE

Cyber-security is a significant risk faced by all organisations that have an online presence or use the internet for communication. When an email account is compromised, either internally or externally, it can cause significant financial damage in instances where the same or similar vendor email addresses are used to request advanced payments and change of bank account information to diverted illicit accounts used to launder the proceeds of the fraud. The criminal can take advantage of this situation when the requirement is urgent and normal checks are dropped or missed. Some of the indicators[8] in this type of fraud might include:

1. unexplained urgency to complete orders
2. last-minute changes in bank account and payment transfer information
3. last-minute changes in established communication platforms or email account addresses
4. communications only by email and refusal to communicate via telephone or online voice or video platforms
5. requests for advanced payment of services when not previously required
6. requests from employees to change direct deposit information

---

[8] https://www.fbi.gov/news/pressrel/press-releases/fbi-anticipates-rise-in-business-email-compromise-schemes-related-to-the-covid-19-pandemic

CHAPTER 6
Organised Crime Groups' Infiltration of Procurement

The scale of organised crime, the routes they take and the level of infiltration of public procurement differs in each country, and thus the risks and methodologies highlighted will differ in each country. However, in outlining these areas of risk and methodologies, it is recommended that a formal risk assessment is carried out on public procurement systems to identify the level of risk and improper influence that is faced within public procurement from organised crime groups (OCGs). This can be done as a stand-alone risk assessment or can be incorporated within an organisation's procurement fraud and corruption risk review.

OCGs, in their attempts to acquire and launder the proceeds of their criminal enterprises, use several global routes and methods to move and hide the origins of their finances, including their attempt to legitimise these illicit funds. OCGs are generally involved in more than one illegal business activity to maximise the profits from their illegal enterprise. Divergence into legal business is not only an additional revenue stream for OCGs, and significantly profitable, but can also be a method of obfuscating illicit activities and can provide the opportunity to mix illicit and licit revenues.

Figures

It is difficult to quantify the scale of the global risk from organised crime and organised crime infiltration of public procurement. A number of examples give an indication to the scale of organised crime risk and the financial impact.

1. Law enforcement[9] agencies across the UK estimate that there are 39,000 people involved in more than 5,800 groups ('Tackling Serious and Organised Crime: A Local Response', Local Government Association).
2. To understand the size of this phenomenon, as an example, in Italy it is estimated that illegal proceeds amount around to €25.7 billion (equivalent to 1.7% of Italy's GDP).[10]
3. A report from the charity Focus on Labour Exploitation (FLEX)[11] found that 50% of migrant workers from Eastern Europe had no written contract, with 36% saying they had not been paid for work completed or did not understand all the deductions on their payslips.
4. Serious and organised waste crime is estimated to cost the UK economy at least £600 million a year, and an independent review commissioned by the Home Office in 2018[12] found that perpetrators are often involved in other serious criminal activities, including large-scale fraud and in some cases modern slavery.

---

[9] https://www.local.gov.uk/sites/default/files/documents/tackling-serious-and-orga-44a.pdf
[10] Transcrime and Università Cattolica di Milano (2013)
[11] https://www.labourexploitation.org
[12] https://assets.publishing.service.gov.uk/government/uploads/system/uploads/attachment_data/file/756526/waste-crime-review-2018-final-report.pdf

Defining organised crime groups

The United Nations Convention against Transnational Organised Crime defines an organised criminal group as:

1. a structured group of three or more persons
2. existing for a period and acting in concert with the aim of committing one or more serious crimes or offences
3. obtaining, directly or indirectly, a financial or other material benefit

Interpol[13] states that as a general rule organised criminal networks are involved in many different types of criminal activities spanning several countries. These activities may include trafficking people, drugs, illicit goods and weapons, armed robbery, counterfeiting and money laundering.

Impact

This section will highlight the various risks that can be introduced from OCG infiltration of public procurement. However, four risk areas that can have a direct or indirect impact of contracting with companies linked to OCGs include:

1. environmental, which includes the illegal dumping of hazardous waste
2. financial, which includes low bids to win a contract using various methodologies to inflate the value of a contract and share profits of corruption, or the use of bribery to win contracts where the works provided will be inferior
3. quality[14]—as an example, in areas of Italy where there is a heavy mafia and organised crime presence, scores of bridges and tunnels are under investigation concerning the use of unfortified concrete. This material contains higher amounts of sand and water and a lower proportion of concrete than regular cement, and as such poses a risk to the integrity of infrastructure or construction projects
4. modern-day slavery, which includes organised crime and the use of these individuals across the global supply chain, including manufacturing and construction

Enablers—why is it made possible?

There are many common and differing reasons why OCGs can infiltrate public procurement.

1. Globally, there can be an information-sharing disconnect between **law enforcement** agencies whose role it is to identify and respond to the national threat from organised crime.
2. In their approach to protect **sensitive data,** which might include covert methods of collecting information and its sources on OCGs' transition into legitimate business by law enforcement organisations, information isn't shared with procurement or compliance professionals in the public sector or government organisation to help them assess procurement fraud and corruption risk.
3. A lack of training and knowledge of procurement fraud and corruption risk in government and public sectors, including OCG infiltration of public procurement.
4. Varying levels of vendor vetting and contract management to verify OCG risk.

---

[13] https://www.interpol.int/Crimes/Organized-crime
[14] https://www.raconteur.net/business-innovation/organised-crime-construction

Organisational enablers

The culmination of various factors may enable organised crime business to move into public procurement contracts with minimal difficulty.

RESOURCE

Risk can arise in situations where there is a lack of knowledge or expertise in a role and an inadequate number of resources to protect and manage an organisation's procurement and compliance processes. An organisation can also be affected when there is an urgent requirement or impact from a national or global crisis and resources are diverted or reduced and the current supply chain can't meet a requirement.

COMPLIANCE

Weak compliance procedures or resources within an organisation, including a lack of understanding of an insider threat or corruption risk, can make the infiltration of procurement less difficult for OCGs. What **hurdles** and **guardianship** does the organisation have in place and how does this impact the counter-fraud environment and culture?

PRESSURE

The internal and external pressures—particularly when there are urgent requirements and deadlines, financial constraints and staff reduction—may mean that normal controls are reduced. Any impact on resources, compliance and pressures may increase the **opportunity** for organised crime.

DEMAND

Demand that can be connected to increased pressure—or if there is an urgent requirement—can create circumstances in which normal procurement routes and procedures are relaxed. This can include external or political influence in which organised crime can infiltrate public procurement. The Covid-19 global pandemic and competing international healthcare systems has highlighted how easily organised crime can introduce inferior or substituted products into global supply chains, including using the online marketplace to receive payments for fictitious personal protection equipment and counterfeit pharmaceutical products.

Defining corruption

Transparency International (TI)[15] defines corruption as the 'abuse of entrusted power for private gain'. It can be classified as grand, petty and political, depending on the amounts of money lost and the sector in which it occurs. Corruption is generally identified with a public or government official who requests, receives or agrees to receive a kickback to facilitate, as an example, the award of a contract. Bribery is linked to business and the offer, promise or giving of a pecuniary advantage, as an example, to gain or retain a contract. However, within business-to-business procurement or projects, the corrupt act of requesting or receiving a bribe is common, and, as such, corruption here is described as the insider threat and the act of bribery as the external threat.

PETTY CORRUPTION

Petty corruption refers to the everyday abuse of entrusted power by low- and mid-level public officials in their interactions with members of the public, who are often trying to access basic goods or services in places like hospitals, schools, police departments, and other agencies.

---

[15] https://www.transparency.org/what-is-corruption

GRAND CORRUPTION

Grand corruption consists of acts committed at a high level of government that distort policies or the central functioning of the state, enabling leaders to benefit at the expense of the public good.

POLITICAL CORRUPTION

Political corruption is a manipulation of policies, institutions and rules or procedures in the allocation of resources and financing by political decision makers who abuse their position to sustain their power, status and wealth.

The UK Home Office describes corruption as a 'widely used tactic'[16] of organised crime. Due to the covert nature of corruption, it is difficult to quantify the level and degree of corruption.

The value of corruption to organised crime groups

Depending on the activities of an OCG, the use of corruption can have significant value, which may include:

1. facilitating the operation of illegal markets, including across borders
2. obtaining information on investigations
3. obtaining information on operations or competitors
4. protection for continued illegal activities
5. targeting politicians, government administration, police, customs, judiciary and private companies to achieve their aims

It is reported that the most widespread and systematic forms of corruption targeted by organised crime are associated with the **low-ranking employees** of police and public administration. Organised crime may also target tax administrations, financial regulators and any other regulatory bodies that might impact criminal activities but in a less systematic and significant way.[17]

Organised crime tactics

To facilitate an environment of corruption and ensure they achieve their business requirement, the OCG can use many additional tactics.

BRIBERY

As already discussed, most bribes are made to low-ranking government or public officials. Europol[18] highlights that criminal groups also use this approach to obtain information or influence the bid evaluation within public service tenders and that this methodology is notable in the energy, construction, information technology and waste management sectors.

FRAUD SCHEMES

OCG fraud schemes can be diverse in nature and target several government organisations at the same time. However, when we examine procurement risk, a number of approaches can be taken, including

---

[16] https://assets.publishing.service.gov.uk/government/uploads/system/uploads/attachment_data/file/97823/organised-crime-strategy.pdf
[17] Gounev (2010)
[18] https://www.europol.europa.eu/crime-areas-and-statistics/crime-areas/economic-crime#:~:text=Organised%20crime%20groups%20are%20increasingly%20involved%20in%20fraud,submit%20fraudulent%20applications%20for%20EU%20grants%20or%20tenders.

using legal companies to bid on public sector procurement and turning to the online sale of counterfeit or fictitious goods. This was evident during the Covid-19 pandemic, when governments were actively searching globally for finite PPE and payments were made for inferior or counterfeit products or PPE that was never received.

EXTORTION

The use of extortion to obtain property or other financial benefits using violence or threats of future physical or reputational harm, demanding money or contracts with menaces, including blackmail. In most cases, bribery or fraud schemes are opportunistic white-collar crimes by individuals rather than OCGs.

Organised crime illicit activity

To achieve the aims of the OCG, there are many examples of the OCG's illicit behaviour:[19]

1. Low-value bribery (the most common corruption approach is to low-ranking public officials)
2. Indirect access by OCG leadership (usually, the leader of the OCG employs an agent to deal with public officials)
3. 'Pantouflage', in which corrupt public officials are rewarded by gaining a position in the private sector
4. Promises of jobs
5. Offers of houses and properties at advantageous prices
6. Support for lifestyle weaknesses identified while observing the targeted public servants
7. The exploitation of family ties
8. Threats of violence intended to intimidate those who have been corrupted

In many respects, the methods of bribery and corruption are no different to white-collar crime and the approach that businesses take in illicitly obtaining contracts. One key difference is the use of and escalation into violence—or threat of violence—and blackmail.

Corruption within procurement

Within the UK HM Government report 'Local to Global: Reducing the Risk from Organised Crime',[20] in describing the corruption of public officials, it states that OCGs will seek to make use of links to law enforcement and prisons, the legal and accountancy professions and those in the private sector.

Within public procurement, institutionalised grand corruption[21] refers to the:

1. allocation and performance of public contracts, by
2. bending universalistic rules of open and fair access to government contracts to benefit a closed network, while
3. denying access to all others

---

[19] *Understanding and Responding to Serious and Organised Crime Involvement in Public Sector Corruption*, Russell G Smith, Tony Oberman and Georgina Fuller (2018)

[20] https://assets.publishing.service.gov.uk/government/uploads/system/uploads/attachment_data/file/97823/organised-crime-strategy.pdf

[21] https://papers.ssrn.com/sol3/papers.cfm?abstract_id=2891017 ('A Comprehensive Review of Objective Corruption Proxies in Public Procurement: Risky Actors, Transactions and Vehicles of Rent Extraction', Governance Transparency Institute, 2016)

Such corruption may involve bribery and the transfer of large cash amounts as kickbacks, but it is more typically conducted through:

1. the use of broker firms, agents and intermediaries—including lawyers, accountants and real estate agents—to hide the criminal source of funds
2. the use of sub-contracts and sub-contractors to avoid the vetting process and hide company ownership and the method of bribe payment
3. offshore companies, to hide the beneficial ownership and bribe payment
4. bogus consultancy contracts, where no services were provided but were used as a route to pay bribes

The World Bank[22] defines corruption in public procurement as an 'action to steer a contract to the favoured bidder without detection'. This insider threat can manipulate the procurement process and award of a contract through different routes. Examples of these methods include:

1. avoiding competition through unjustified single sourcing or direct contracting of a contract
2. favouring a certain bidder by tailoring specifications
3. sharing inside information

Organised crime supply chain

When examining the risk of supply chain infiltration, several areas stand out—specifically:

*   manufacturing
*   transportation
*   landlords
*   sales

In the same way that counterfeiters' supply chains can be broken down into these four areas, organised crime can be much the same.

Manufacture

At this stage, manufacture provides multiple opportunities for organised crime to infiltrate the supply chain.

1. Ingredients, parts and components to enter the supply chain of otherwise legitimate products.
2. Products, such as poor-quality, counterfeit personal protection and equipment and pharmaceuticals are created, marketed and sold.
3. Introducing slavery or trafficked individuals into the process to reduce the total cost of manufacture.

Transport operators

Counterfeit and other illicit goods depend on land, air and sea shipping and transportation services to cross borders and reach foreign markets. While parcel trade has long been a common feature of international trade, the widespread adoption of digital technologies is now enabling firms to internationalise their operations at a lower cost and vary routes and transportation methods to elude law enforcement, tax and customs officials.

---

[22] World bank (2009)

<u>Landlords</u>

As landlords are generally not involved in the inspection of their premises once rented out, they may unwittingly allow illicit activities to go on unchecked and undetected. Landlords may knowingly or unknowingly rent the space needed for one or more activities that could include providing a place to manufacture, store or sell illicit products.

<u>Sales</u>

Criminal groups continue to diversify ways in which they sell and introduce their product into legitimate supply chains.

1. Landlords may provide a place to sell illicit products.
2. The greater use of websites and parcel delivery.
3. The In Our Sites joint international operation, Europol's Intellectual Property Crime Coordinated Coalition (IPC3),[23] has seized 33,654 domain names distributing counterfeit and pirated items online. The websites distributed items such as counterfeit pharmaceuticals, pirated films, television shows, music, software, electronics, and other bogus products. The joint international operation also involved the US National Intellectual Property Rights Coordination Center and law enforcement authorities from 26 countries, including the EU Member States and third parties[2], which was facilitated by Interpol.

INTERMEDIARIES

Intermediaries can be involved in various aspects of a legitimate, inferior or counterfeit product supply chain to help introduce these products into a legitimate supply chain. Increasingly, organised crime networks are introducing counterfeit elements through intermediaries who are involved in producing, distributing and selling a product, from raw materials through to final product.

Counterfeiting and the links to organised crime

The OCGs that have diversified into the field of counterfeit products do not use counterfeiting as their sole method of obtaining illicit funds, but as an attractive route for obtaining additional revenues. Reasons for an OCG's move into counterfeiting might consist of the following:

1. Trafficking in counterfeit goods offers criminals a complementary source of income and a tool to launder proceeds derived from various crimes.
2. Proceeds from other crimes have been used by OCGs to finance their counterfeiting businesses.
3. The profitability from counterfeiting has been estimated as similar or even higher than the trade in narcotics.
4. Public perception is less negative, risks are lower and penalties are generally less than other crimes they may be engaged in.

How corruption is used

Corruption in its various forms can greatly facilitate counterfeiting and its criminal activities and supply chain. Bribery of public servants can enable:

1. the import and transit of counterfeit products—including movement across international borders—that would otherwise have been seized

---

[23] https://www.europol.europa.eu/activities-services/europol-in-action/operations/operation-in-our-sites-ios

2. the issuance of visas or work permits by corrupt officials, which may also allow criminal actors to legally establish companies involved in intellectual property rights (IPR) crime
3. a network of brokers or agents to use corrupt practices or networks to infiltrate the legitimate supply chain, especially during distribution and sales
4. owners of legitimate businesses to cooperate with criminal groups along the supply chain

Why organised crime groups move into legal business

With the increase in OCG engagement and infiltration of public sector procurement through their investment and acquisition of legitimate companies, in addition to the access to an additional revenue stream that could be significant, particularly within government projects, some scholars have highlighted that illicit investment by OCGs in legal companies can be for a specific purpose or benefit:

1. Concealment of criminal activities (mainly money laundering)
2. Control of the territory
3. Social consensus
4. Profit (and/or income) maximisation
5. Cultural/personal reasons (i.e. criminals investing in certain businesses because it is close to their culture, educational background, family tradition, status and prestige)
6. Targeting businesses in economic difficulties to facilitate the infiltration process, since the owners of the companies are eager to sell their shares before leading their business to bankruptcy[24]

Organised crime proceeds invested in the legitimate economy

To examine and identify opportunities for OCGs to infiltrate public procurement, we must first understand which businesses are invested in or associated with OCGs. The cash-based industry is still a significant area where their illicit proceeds are laundered. However, with criminal links and the use of professional services, such as lawyers and accountants, the types of companies is diverse and can incorporate:

1. bars and restaurants
2. construction, within the infrastructure sector[25]—it is estimated that in certain circumstances the financial loss incurred due to corruption can range between 10% and 30% of publicly funded construction projects
3. wholesale and retail trade (especially of clothing and food products)
4. transportation
5. hotels and real estate, traditional sectors of infiltration
6. renewable energy
7. waste and scrap management, waste management[26] contracts,[27] identified through illegal fly-tipping (local government and law enforcement contracts)
8. logistics (incorporating other areas of business, such as people trafficking)
9. money transfer businesses, slot machines, betting and gaming
10. healthcare systems

[24] Berlusconi (2015)
[25] https://www.europarl.europa.eu/RegData/etudes/STUD/2016/579319/EPRS_STU%282016%29579319_EN.pdf
[26] https://www.gov.uk/government/news/clock-is-ticking-for-waste-criminals-as-new-taskforce-launched
[27] https://www.spectator.co.uk/article/What-is-organised-crime-doing-disposing-of-rubbish

White-collar crime

Reportedly coined in 1939, the term white-collar crime is now synonymous with the full range of financial crime committed by business and government professionals. These crimes are characterised by:

1. deceit, concealment or violation of trust, and
2. not being dependent on the application or threat of physical force or violence
3. the motivation behind these crimes being financial
4. obtaining or avoiding losing money, property, or services or to securing a personal or business advantage[28]

White-collar crime links to organised crime

White-collar crime can include fraud, bribery, blackmail, counterfeiting, embezzlement, forgery, insider trading and money laundering, often with a nexus to organised crime activities that are international, national or regional in scope. Organised crime[29] is distinguished from white-collar crime (and from commercial and public corruption) because rather than a deviation from lawful activity, it is a continuing criminal enterprise designed to profit primarily from crime.

CARTELS

When firms in the same market engage in a business cartel and control competition between them by fixing prices, sharing markets or rigging tendering procedures, on occasion business cartels can involve OCGs. The actions in this type of interaction might include:

1. making use of the violent reputation provided by criminal groups to control the market
2. controlling the companies involved in the cartel, including the compliance of firms to the existing cartel agreements
3. preventing outsiders of the cartel from entering the market through threats or other illicit means
4. the use of sophisticated administration and shadow bookkeeping

BID RIGGING AND CARTELS

The approach of cartels targeting public procurement is the collusion between companies to control contract award and the market and agree which company will win the contract. OCGs can be used to control the market or ensure compliance with agreed practices and conduct by colluding companies.

MOTIVATION

It has been asserted that organised criminals focus their attention primarily on sectors with a high and immediate return on investments, with risk minimisation, and mainly target healthcare, private clinics and the treatment of urban and toxic waste.

There are various reasons why criminal groups target the public work sector—specifically, what public sector procurement and projects can offer, including:

1. high values and profits that come from public works
2. the investigation of criminal activity within public contracts being difficult to carry out and harder to detect and prove compared to illicit activity, such as drug trafficking

---

[28] Fbi.gov
[29] Albanese (2015): Simpson (2013)

3. weaknesses and inefficiencies of the public administration, especially in certain countries
4. criminal infiltration having strategic importance for strengthening the relationships with politicians and public administrators

How criminals infiltrate public procurement

OCGs infiltrate public procurement because of the attraction and opportunity to earn high revenues. It is estimated that the cost of corruption risk in the European Union public procurement[30] is approximately €5 billion per year. Two areas outline the OCGs' approach to corruption:

1. Opportunistic—usually carried out on an irregular basis by individuals when an opportunity arises and can be taken advantage of
2. Organised—a systemic approach that forms part of a pattern of offending by OCGs and involves collective action by group members seeking to minimise the risk of detection by acting in a planned and coordinated way

Covid-19 use of opportunity

During the global response to Covid-19, there were several patterns and incidents where OCGs developed their operations and targeted public procurement. Due to restrictions placed on travel, meetings and work locations and the impact of urgent procurement, OCGs changed their tactics to meet the opportunity and drop in government control measures. Some of these areas included:

1. infiltration of the healthcare system, which involved counterfeit and inferior products or illegally diverted pharmaceuticals—a lucrative criminal industry that could be worth as much as $431 billion annually[31]
2. a significant increase in online purchasing and sales opportunities for counterfeit, inferior and fictitious medical products and pharmaceuticals
3. cyber-crime emerging rapidly as a risk area that could have long-term implications for the growth of criminal markets
4. incidents of smuggling and theft of medical supplies—including inferior and counterfeit products and personal protection equipment—that were misdescribed to avoid customs checks and were intercepted by customs authorities

Research carried out by the United Nations Office of Drugs and Crime (UNODC)[32] and the impact from OCGs found that economic sectors vulnerable to infiltration by OCGs due to the financial distress caused by the Covid-19 crisis included:

1. retail and marketplaces
2. tourism and hospitality
3. transportation
4. arts, entertainment and recreation

It was further identified that economic sectors vulnerable to OCG infiltration, because of the opportunities to benefit from the Covid-19 crisis, included:

1. logistics and e-commerce
2. wholesale trade in medical products

---

[30] https://www.rand.org/pubs/research_reports/RR1483.html
[31] https://globalinitiative.net/wp-content/uploads/2020/03/GI-TOC-Crime-and-Contagion-The-impact-of-a-pandemic-on-organized-crime-1.pdf
[32] The impact of Covid-19 on organised crime, UNODC

3. wholesale trade in pharmaceutical products
4. food retail trade
5. cleaning services, waste management and funeral services

Areas targeted

The relationship between organised crime[33] and its use of corruption to infiltrate public procurement can be targeted at several areas and levels of an organisation's management:

1. Low levels of government agencies
2. Having low-ranking state officials on the organised criminal payroll
3. Infiltration of the managerial domain to favour the operations of the criminal group
4. Head of agencies responsible for fighting organised crime related activities
5. State capture that influences national policies by criminal groups, who are then able to bias law making, law enforcement and judicial decisions

Political and personal connections

OCGs can target politicians and senior government officials in the same way that other corrupt actors do to abuse their position of power and influence for illicit gain. There are many routes this can take.

1. Direct personal ties through friendship or membership in associations between a political office holder and a bidding firm owner or executive
2. Indirect personal ties, such as geographical proximity between a political office holder and bidding firm owner or executive who helps facilitate a personal relationship
3. Revolving door political officeholder(s)—moving between public office and bidding firms or private sector into public office
4. Political party donations—bidding company or individual associated with a bidding firm donating to a party or an individual's electoral campaign, including political donations linked to a bidding firm
5. Lobbying activity by or linked to a bidding firm targeting a political office holder's involvement in or link to lobbying and area of influence

Corruption and the insider threat within procurement

The areas of the procurement process that can be influenced by a corrupt relationship will likely depend on whether it is low-level or grand corruption and their interaction within a contract or project or their ability to influence decision making within the onboarding, the procurement route or the selection and award process.

LOW-LEVEL CORRUPTION

Low-level corruption can still impact the procurement route and tender process. However, depending on the role of the corrupt individual, they have the potential to manipulate any stage of the procurement life cycle because of their direct involvement with the process.

GRAND CORRUPTION

Corrupt relationships and the abuse of power and influence by the political elite and government leaders generally manipulate the award of contracts in two key areas—specifically, the direct award

---

[33] Buscaglia and van Dijk (2003) identified five levels of infiltration

of contracts and the manipulation of the tender process—to ensure that the agreed company is awarded a contract. Additional risk areas where grand corruption is involved might include senior government officials signing or approving licenses or protecting the contractor where illicit conduct is suspected.

Organised crime networks

In addition to the bribery of public officials in key positions, OCGs can penetrate an organisation's procurement system in both the public and private sectors by placing OCG operatives in a management position that can influence procurement decisions and divert resources.

Cartels and corruption

In addition to the manipulation of the bidding process by cartels, a corrupt relationship with a low-level official involved in the procurement process through bid manipulation can ensure that the bid rigging approach is successful. It is also of note that where a business bribes a government official to obtain or retain a contract, it is likely that the financial loss of the payment will be recovered within the price of the contract, thus there is no value for money within the contract price. Additionally, there is no guarantee that the business would have won the tender had they competed for the goods, works or services or whether their product is of satisfactory quality.

Risk indicators within the submission phase

There are many risk indicators where tender conditions are tailored to fit a specific company. Within the bid submission phase of the procurement process, common methodologies[34] used by organised crime and corrupt relationships include:

1. single bid contracts, where only one company responds—has there been internal manipulation of the process or is there external influence by the cartel?
2. a call for tender not being published in the official journal, reducing the opportunity for legitimate companies to reply
3. procedure type (open procedure or restricted procedure)
4. length of submission period—number of days between the publication of a call for tenders and the submission deadline
5. call for tender modification

What is clear from these methods is that they are no different to other typologies used by companies or an insider intent on committing fraud. When assessing an organisation's process for procurement fraud and corruption, risk from OCGs should be considered.

Risk indicators within the assessment phase

There are many risk indicators within the assessment phase of the procurement bidding process. However, common methodologies used by organised crime and corrupt relationships include:

1. exclusion of all but one bid
2. invalidated procedures—no contract awarded in the selection procedure, or the contract awarded in the procedure is invalidated but relaunched

---

[34] How Criminals Infiltrate Public Procurement: Organised Crime and Corruption in Legal Markets and Public Sectors, Caterina Mazza (2016)

3. the length of the decision period—the number of working days between the submission deadline and announcing the contract award
4. unit price percentage deviation of standardised unit compared to private market price or lowest public procurement price

Emerging trends

OCGs continue to look at the opportunity to hide illicit proceeds and develop new areas of illicit and licit business:

1. Money laundering by alternative banking platforms and the use of new technologies
2. Increased regional, national and international dimensions to their business
3. Greater exploitation of legitimate markets—as an example, importation of tobacco and alcohol—and bypassing tax laws
4. Increased use of anonymising IT, communication technology and internet sites and solutions
5. Increased use of front companies—as an example, high street nail salons—to act as a veil of legitimacy over the criminal enterprise (cash-based business)

UK local government has been highlighted as at risk of becoming victims of serious and organised crime. Councils are particularly at risk of fraud, including procurement fraud, bribery and corruption, and third-party actors unknowingly participating in serious and organised crime.

To fully understand the diversity of procurement fraud and corruption risk that may impact an organisation, a greater understanding of how OCGs and their potential to infiltrate legitimate supply chains are an important part of any risk assessment and mitigation approach.

CHAPTER 7
Risk Areas Within Projects

Due to the high values involved, the significant levels of procurement, the volume of invoices, limited administration and compliance resources—including minimal counter-fraud controls—projects can be a high-risk target by procurement fraud. In addition to the procurement fraud risk already highlighted in the previous chapters, within projects there are many additional areas of potential risk and instances where individuals can influence decision making and project outcomes. A mitigation approach should consider areas of risk that include project planning, areas of project manipulation, project management, risk reports and support roles.

Creating a project plan and procurement plan can be integral within projects to ensure that it meets the outcomes anticipated. However, it is rare that an counter-fraud plan for each project is created in the planning stage to ensure that potential risks are mitigated.

Within the initial project appraisal and feasibility stage, where an assessment is made of potential solutions for a current need or problem, fictitious, exaggerated or ineffective requirements or overstated benefits and underestimated costs can be introduced with the illicit aim of increasing project values, agreeing future fraud activities or diverting project funds.

Project planning

Within the planning stage and before project commencement there can be many opportunities for fraud, including designing fraud opportunities into a project. Such examples might include:

1. deliberately designing a project to fail in order to allow the monies involved to be diverted (a business case can be created where the justification and business benefits are false or inflated to incorporate a level of fraud, theft and corruption)
2. the initial design of a project being created around a vendor's expertise or product or details of the design or specification being improperly disclosed during the bidding process to influence the technical submission with a competitive tender
3. calculations or projections being deliberately inflated to hide an element of fraud or deliberately being kept low to give the appearance of value, with additional costs and variations being illicitly introduced during the lifetime of the project
4. fraud being introduced during the planning stage—if authority levels are not correctly introduced, reducing the level of oversight—that will be carried out during the project
5. deliberately withholding areas of maintenance or other future costs within the initial financial planning and calculations to give the appearance of value for money, where additional costs will be added through contract variation within the project
6. more than one budget or cost centre being used to hide the total value of a project or level of funds defrauded

Project risk framework

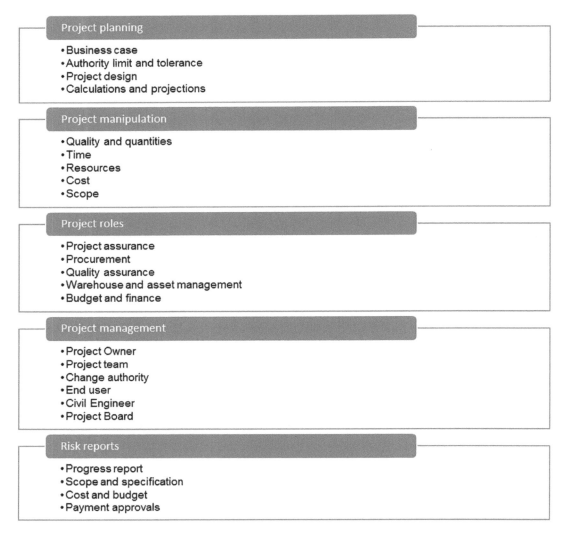

Project planning
- Business case
- Authority limit and tolerance
- Project design
- Calculations and projections

Project manipulation
- Quality and quantities
- Time
- Resources
- Cost
- Scope

Project roles
- Project assurance
- Procurement
- Quality assurance
- Warehouse and asset management
- Budget and finance

Project management
- Project Owner
- Project team
- Change authority
- End user
- Civil Engineer
- Project Board

Risk reports
- Progress report
- Scope and specification
- Cost and budget
- Payment approvals

Project manipulation

In addition to the procurement fraud typologies already mentioned, there are additional areas within projects that can be susceptible to fraud risk.

1. To build in a level of fraud through a badly written **scope** during the planning stage of a project where additional requirements or changes will be needed during the contract.
2. False billing for **resources**, which includes using higher rates or invoicing for scarce resources such as project managers or civil engineers across numerous projects or where consultants are used—projects are billed for the cost of a senior consultant, and more junior consultants are substituted to undertake work—or billing for ghost employees.
3. Using counterfeit, substituted or **inferior-quality** products or materials to maximise profits by the contractor during the lifetime of the project.
4. Exploitation of **quantities**, either within the initial design and assessment of material requirement, to be able to complete a project, or inflated invoicing for materials used. Workforce quantities can be manipulated either by inflating the numbers used or by decreasing the numbers below the required levels within a contract and invoicing for the full amount.
5. The manipulation of **time** during a project, through deliberate delays by the client, can incur additional resources and compensation to complete a project on time.

6. The **cost** of a project can also be manipulated through hiding total costs within other budgets or cost centres. A lack of segregation of duties, control measures, audit, and monitoring can facilitate the misuse of areas such as urgent requirements, which impact the total cost.

Research[35] that focused on estimates of costs and demand associated with major infrastructure projects spanning 258 projects in 20 countries over five continents found that nine out of ten projects have a significant cost overrun. They argue that 'the practice of deliberate, strategic misrepresentation of costs and benefits comes into focus as a form of corruption alongside bid rigging and collusion'.

Project fraud risk

It is important to assess the project fraud and corruption risk at the planning stage and ensure that the procurement fraud typologies and control measures are considered as part of this assessment. There are several common examples of fraud risks within projects.

1. Difficult to control segregation of duties, where an individual who can identify a new requirement can procure the item and sign off that the work has been completed or the goods have been received.
2. High use of temporary staff or consultants, if monitoring is not in place, may lead to a false and inflated invoicing for resources.
3. Vague consultancy arrangements or bought-in services supported by generic invoices that do not record or itemise the goods, works or services provided.
4. Sub-contractors can be hidden when there is no contractual requirement to request authorisation for their use. Such an approach can be used by a contractor as part of a bid rigging scheme or as a method of paying bribes when the corrupt individual is linked to the sub-contractor, such as the owner or shareholder.
5. Scarce resources, such as project managers, civil engineers and quantity surveyors, are used between projects and billed for by falsely inflating the number of resources available onsite for each project.
6. Project managers or related staff are corruptly induced or pressured to sign off substandard or incomplete work.
7. Where no audit is conducted, or only carried out at the end of a project, it creates an opportunity for the fraud to be hidden and, on many occasions, will likely never be identified.
8. No contractor staff monitoring, which creates an opportunity for false billing and fictitious timesheets, including an inability to verify the accuracy of the information provided.
9. Hidden fraud within turnkey projects through the introduction of inferior quality or a change in specification.
10. Misuse of urgent requirements and single source procurement to introduce fraud.
11. Inadequate resources allocated to contract management, which ensures that compliance staff cannot accurately assess all invoice submissions.
12. There are many examples globally of projects that have been deliberately designed to fail[36] in order to illicitly divert the project budget and funds.

AD HOC AND EMERGENCY WORKS

In projects, it is not unusual to come across the need for ad hoc or emergency works—specifically, work that is not planned and where issues are identified that may cause delay or risk within a project if identified work is not completed. Where there is a lack of transparency and an oversight in these

---

[35] Flyvbjerg & Molloy (2011)
[36] https://www.giaba.org/media/f/1011_Money-Laundering-Related-Public-Procurement-Fraud-Formatted.pdf

areas, the process may create an opportunity for planned fraud to be introduced into a project. Such indicators of fraud might include:

1. numerous emergency works in the same area, which might indicate a fictitious requirement
2. unusual time of works when completion cannot be verified
3. materials used, or completed work not fit for purpose
4. vague work requirements or unclear invoices that have not been verified as complete
5. inspection records missing or falsified
6. out-of-contract work

RISK MANAGEMENT

Roles that identify or authorise additional works or changes to the scope of a project can be the target of fraud and bribery.

1. An **end-user** can influence a project and its outcomes by introducing additional requirements within the lifetime of the project, which creates additional profit for the contractor.
2. The role of the **project manager** can include the overall responsibility for the successful initiation, planning, design, execution, monitoring, controlling and closure of a project; activity and resource planning; controlling time management; cost estimating and developing the budget; analysing and managing project risk; monitoring progress; managing reports and necessary documentation; controlling quality; and working with vendors. A project manager is at high risk of bribery because of the integral role they play within a project, which can influence many areas of a project, including signing off works as they are completed.
3. Where a **civil engineer** is used within a project, their role might include analysing the site location and the surrounding area through search and investigation, verifying its feasibility for construction purposes; designing a plan outlining the key variables and what needs to be changed before the construction; developing a detailed design layout; and monitoring the staff onsite and keeping an open dialogue with architects, consultants and sub-contractors. Should any issues arise, they have the responsibility of resolving them. In this high-risk role, they are in a position to create and sign off fictitious requirements or work that hasn't been completed.
4. The **project owner,** like all other project roles, may be able to influence decisions within the project scope and specification.
5. A member of the **project board** may influence decisions around changes of scope or other change orders.
6. Where an organisation does not have a **change authority** or roles in place to manage and authorise the change process, there may be a higher risk of fraud being introduced into the project, where numerous changes are made to the project.

RISK REPORTS

Within project monitoring and control, there can be several ways in which assessment and reporting of project progress and risk are conducted, including at key stages within the project. The flow of information and transparency within a project can assist the measurement of fraud and corruption risk, and where there is an inability to check or verify information or invoices, there may be an increased opportunity for fraud risk to be introduced.

1. Where an individual deliberately **under-reports** the project cost to give the appearance of strong management and good governance—the impact of this falsehood may not be understood until the end of a project or until an audit is carried out.

2. Instances where changes are made within the **scope** and specification of a project without the knowledge of the client or authorising body.

3. In circumstances when there is a significant volume of invoices and limited resources to verify before **payment approval** that work has been completed and is of the specification and quality requested, or instances when resources are not provided and are being invoiced for.

4. In circumstances where there is limited financial reporting or where **budgets** are overestimated or payments are made against other budgets or cost centres to hide the true value of the project, thus the true level of fraud may not be determined.

5. **Over-reporting** the progress of a project can allow for additional or landmark payments to a contractor in meeting agreed timescales.

SUPPORT ROLES

In addition to the positions and functions that have already been mentioned, several roles are important to support the administration, completion and governance of a project. Where specific roles are under-resourced, or there is a lack of expertise in the field, there can be a greater opportunity for individuals to take advantage of procedure, control or resource weakness.

1. The lack of adequate **procurement** resources or expertise in a project. Due to the significant volume of procurement that can be required, procurement control measures or governance may be reduced, which can enable various typologies of procurement fraud.

2. The limited oversight within projects of product failure and **maintenance** regimes may create an environment where fictitious works are created or counterfeit or inferior products are introduced.

3. The lack of strong **asset management** and asset tracking in a project may allow for large-scale theft to occur, which might create circumstances where assets are stolen for the benefit of a supplier and then resold to the organisation through normal procurement routes.

4. Limited **financial** resources and inadequate verification of work completion or services and materials provided before payment can create an environment for fraud to develop. Examples may include invoices received that are vague or billing for high levels of temporary staff that cannot be checked against timesheets or onsite verification of attendance.

5. The retention and analysis of **quality-assurance** data is an important part of project assurance and the identification of procurement fraud risk. If products or equipment start failing, it may be an indicator that there is product substitution or counterfeit or inferior products.

6. Limited project assurance, including verification of quality, resources and project completion, can create an environment where fraud can be hidden, including poor performance by the contractor, which might indicate that the tender selection and contract award process has been manipulated to award the contract through corruption to a company that is unable to complete the work, or the onboarding measures aren't adequate.

PROJECT AND CONTRACT MANAGEMENT RISK

When examining the post-award procurement or project risks, there are several common risk areas where procurement fraud can occur:

1. A high level of **emergency** works in the same area of a project may indicate that some of these works are fictitious or it may be an indication of a fault with a product or its maintenance. This might suggest that a substandard product was substituted for the genuine product. Are non-urgent works classified as an emergency to expedite the requirement, loosen controls and avoid scrutiny?

2. Procurement on an **ad hoc** basis allows tasks to be done as they are requested—in some cases, without any formal approval process. This approach may also provide little in the way of management or accountability.

3. A significant number of contract **variations** may indicate fraudulent activity, which may be linked to the deliberate inferior design of a project that requires additional design and contract amendments or the creation of a false requirement to divert funds. Additionally, where there is a corruption risk, variations may be added without approval.

4. Where there is no proper oversight of **change orders,** a change order created by a project owner could introduce fraud into the contract through a change in contract values, requirements or timescale.

5. A last minute or unscheduled contractor is brought in to carry out contract variations or change orders.

6. A risk within projects can include the **improper sign-off** of works or timesheets by the project manager for incomplete works or false quantity of resources provided, or to allow for payment of on-time bonuses where a contractor does not meet key milestones or deliverables.

7. A lack of **asset receipt**, management and asset tracking within projects can facilitate large-scale theft and fraud.

8. Where projects are not effectively managed, in addition to the normal typologies of procurement fraud the manipulation of **time, quality, quantity** and **resources** are also common to inflate the cost of a contract or introduce inferior products to inflate contractor profit within the lifetime of the project.

9. The use of **sub-contractors** by the main contractor can hide several fraud or corruption risks—including being part of the initial bid rigging scheme, weakness within the selection process and the main contractor's inability to perform the contract—or a route used to pay bribes where the sub-contractor is not vetted for conflict-of-interest risk.

10. **False claims** are a common method of fraud, including billing for goods, works or services that have not been provided or completed, mischarging of line items or contract rates, or billing for a fictitious requirement.

11. During the contract management phase additional areas of risk might include the manipulation of contract terms and pricing or billing for work that is not covered under the contract.

12. Work or invoicing continues after the contract has expired.

BID RIGGING

Creating a cartel from competing companies can have several financial benefits for a company, including maximising contract profits, stabilising what might be a volatile market and controlling competition to ensure they receive consistent revenues and guaranteed contracts. A company may also receive monies as part of the collusion, where the winning company and lowest bid has inflated their price to include the sharing of profits.

Environment

An environment that is conducive to collusive behaviour, price-fixing and bid rigging is one that provides colluding companies with the opportunity to communicate undetected.[37] Other environmental characteristics might include:

1. regular and recurring procurement that creates an environment for bid rigging to develop and assists in the allocation between colluding companies

---

[37] https://www.oecd.org/competition/cartels/42851044.pdf

2. vendor forums to act as a cover
3. pre-bid meetings or business associations that allow colluding companies to discuss openly without raising suspicion
4. a small number of companies in the market or local area providing the required goods, works or services
5. market traits and competition that put pressure on companies to give the lowest price, or where there is economic uncertainty
6. cartels having a greater opportunity of success where there is a limited bidding pool, poor procurement controls and staff who are ill-equipped to know what pricing to expect or lack an understanding of the product they are contracting
7. cartels being easier to manage when there is a fixed price in a project and more difficult when there is a requirement for a breakdown of pricing, increasing the likelihood of error, particularly where information and mistakes are shared
8. attending the bid opening, which will allow colluding companies to identify non-compliance with their agreement and allow the cartel to punish the company that breaches the agreement

Agreement

To ensure that parties involved in the bid rigging scheme comply with the price fixing, market share or bid rigging, a formal or informal agreement that outlines what is required from each company may be created. Agreed terms might include:

1. not to poach other companies' clients or to agree not to develop business in a particular region or divide their market share
2. fixing or inflating the lowest price of materials sold by companies to ensure that they maximise their profits or to agree on a level of profit to be divided between colluding companies
3. the exchange of competitively sensitive information to monitor individual company activity
4. colluding companies agreeing which company will win a tender or future tenders and which company will act as a sub-contractor
5. which company, if applicable, will draft and share their bid submission details— including pricing and technical information—between the group to ensure that the colluding company submissions are inferior in price, quality or technical ability
6. agreeing on the method in which the companies will manipulate the bidding process to give the appearance of competition
7. restricting the supply of equipment or material on the market to increase the price

Collusion

To ensure a greater opportunity of success for colluding companies and to give the appearance of competition within the bidding process, common bid rigging methodology might include the following:

1. A company may deliberately fail to respond to the bid request or withdraw its bid during the bidding process.
2. A vendor either submits a bid that is much higher than the winning bid or too high to be accepted, is poorly written, does not meet the specification or has additional terms that rule it out in the selection process.
3. Procurement law or organisational bidding procedures may make a stipulation around the complete and clear submission of bid paperwork. This allows a colluding company to make deliberate mistakes or ensure that their bid submission is not complete, so that they are ruled out of the process.

4. The winning bid is awarded to another company within the cartel that was not agreed and the contract winner declines the award or recommends that another company involved in the bidding process should be awarded the contract.
5. A contractor's refusal to bid because of perceived or actual threats from other companies.
6. Use of an association or other third party unknowingly linked to bidding companies to influence contract conditions.

Collusive indicators

The covert nature of corrupt or collusive relationships can make procurement fraud difficult to identify during the procurement life cycle. However, indicators of bid rigging risk and patterns during the tender process might include:

1. the same company always winning a tender in specific types of procurement or projects, or the same company always losing
2. identical mistakes, terminology or pricing, or line items used within vendor bids
3. identical or similar bid submissions, including handwriting, font or use of the same stationery
4. duplicate data on different bids, including sub-contractors, addresses and contact information
5. losing company works as a sub-contractor
6. unqualified bidding company winning the tender
7. poor quality of works or services provided as the contracts are rotated between bid rigging companies
8. bidding companies within the scheme dropping their prices when a new vendor competes
9. the same sub-contractor being used by multiple bidding companies
10. an increase in a company's market share and pricing

CHAPTER 8
Counterfeit Product Risk

Counterfeiting is globally recognised as a significant crime that has grown exponentially over the last 40 years. Counterfeit products have proliferated from inferior-quality toys and knock-off watches to a multi-billion-dollar business that in a growing number of cases is linked to organised crime and the financing of terrorism. The financial impact of counterfeit products is significant, which has been highlighted by several global organisations:

1. The Organisation for Economic Cooperation and Development (OECD) estimated that counterfeit products amount to around 3.3% of global trade, which equates to around $590 billion annually.
2. The OECD 2019[38] estimates imports of counterfeit and pirated products into the European Union as amounting to as much as EUR 121 billion, which represents up to 6.8% of EU imports.
3. The International Anti-Counterfeiting Coalition (IACC) reports[39] that counterfeit product trade has increased from $5.5 billion in 1982 to approximately $600 billion today.
4. It is estimated in the UK that counterfeit trade meant the UK government lost almost £3.8 billion in tax revenue.[40]
5. The WHO estimates that the global sale of counterfeit pharmaceuticals could top $75 billion dollars,[41] a 90% rise in five years.
6. There is increasing evidence of links between counterfeiting and the funding of organised crime and terrorism.

Terminology

To understand the breadth of these illicit goods or materials and product infiltration of an organisation's supply chain, the various product risks must be understood. These include:

1. adulteration—when a component of a legitimate finished product is fraudulent
2. counterfeit—when all aspects of the fraudulent product and package are fully replicated
3. diversion—the sale or distribution of a product outside of the intended market
4. overruns—when a legitimate product is produced in excess of manufacture agreement
5. simulation—when an illegitimate product is designed to look like, and exactly copy, the legitimate product
6. tamper—when legitimate products and packages are used in a fraudulent way
7. theft —when a legitimate product is stolen and passed off as legitimately procured

---

[38] https://euipo.europa.eu/tunnel-web/secure/webdav/guest/document_library/observatory/documents/reports/trends_in_trade_in_counterfeit_and_pirated_goods/trends_in_trade_in_counterfeit_and_pirated_goods_infographics_en.pdf
[39] https://www.iacc.org/
[40] http://www.oecd.org/gov/risk/trade-in-counterfeit-products-and-uk-economy-report-update-2019.pdf
[41] https://www.who.int/bulletin/volumes/88/4/10-020410/en/

Distinguishing counterfeit products

In attempting to distinguish counterfeit products and markets, they can be categorised into two types:

1. Deceptive—when consumers are unaware that they are not purchasing original products and cannot detect them by inspection or inference from the place of the purchase
2. Non-deceptive—when consumers know or strongly suspect they have purchased non-original products

COUNTERFEIT MEDICAL PRODUCTS

The WHO, in defining counterfeit medical products, categorised these risks into three areas:

1. Substandard, also called 'out of specification', are authorised medical products that fail to meet either their quality standards or specifications or both.
2. Unregistered or unlicensed medical products that have not undergone evaluation and/or approval by the National or Regional Regulatory Authority for the market in which they are marketed, distributed or used, subject to permitted conditions under national or regional regulation.
3. Falsified medical products that deliberately or fraudulently misrepresent their identity, composition or source.

COUNTERFEIT AND SUBSTANDARD PHARMACEUTICALS

1. The WHO also defines a counterfeit drug as one that is 'deliberately and fraudulently mislabeled concerning the identity and/or source'.
2. The WHO defines substandard drugs as 'genuine drug products which do not meet quality specifications set for them'. Since counterfeiters seek to maximise profits, most counterfeits would be considered substandard if they were genuine products. Not all substandard drugs represent intentional fraud.

Law, regulation and legal protection

In addition to the criminal laws that cover creating, distributing and selling counterfeit products, other areas can assist the protection of individuals and businesses from the counterfeiter, as outlined by the European Union Intellectual Property Office.

TRADEMARK

A trademark is a distinctive sign that identifies certain goods or services as those produced or provided by a specific person or enterprise. Trademarks may include words, personal names, letters, numerals, figurative elements and combinations of colours, as well as any combination of these signs.

COPYRIGHT

Copyright is a set of exclusive rights, subject to limitations, related to the creative works of authors—the rights about, among others, the reproduction, distribution, translation and adaptation, and public performance.

PATENTS

Patents enable the patent holder to exclude unauthorised parties from making, using, offering for sale, selling or importing the protected inventive subject matter.

INDUSTRIAL DESIGN

If an industrial design was based on the exclusive rights conferred, the right holder can prevent third parties from making, selling or importing articles bearing or embodying a protected design without authorisation.

GLOBAL IMPACT

Cheap copies of products, such as clothing and perfumes, have in many ways made counterfeit products socially acceptable to the public. However, the impact on individuals, government and global business can be significant. In many respects, counterfeiting is about maximising profits, and as such, items that have the potential to be counterfeited are those that an organisation or sector needs to procure in significant numbers. As part of a prevention approach, where organisations consider this view, they can target this type of procured goods and materials for counterfeit risk assessment.

The Aerospace Industry Association, in reporting on counterfeit parts,[42] whether they are electronic, mechanical, or other, adversely affects the US supply chain. Possible impacts may include:

Government

1. National security or civilian safety issues
2. Costs of investigation and enforcement
3. Lost tax revenue due to illegal sales of counterfeit parts

Industry

1. Costs to mitigate the risk
2. Costs to replace failed parts
3. Lost sales, lost brand value, or damage to business image

Consumers

1. Costs when products fail due to lower quality and reliability of counterfeit parts
2. Potential safety concerns

Counterfeit pharmaceutical mortality rates

Due to the scale of the manufacture, the multitude of supply chain routes and transportation methods—including porous borders used to facilitate transit—the impact on global health and mortality cannot be measured. However, in areas where pharmaceuticals are being counterfeited mortality rates are likely significant. The WHO alerts at the beginning of 2020 included:

1. falsified medical products, including in-vitro diagnostics that claim to prevent, detect, treat or cure Covid-19
2. falsified HIV rapid diagnostic tests circulating in the WHO regions of the Americas and Africa
3. falsified antimalarials in West and Central Africa displaying an outdated WHO Essential Drugs Programme logo.

---

[42] https://www.aia-aerospace.org/wp-content/uploads/2016/05/counterfeit-web11.pdf

Impact of counterfeit pharmaceuticals

The harm from counterfeit pharmaceuticals can be significant, and depending on the product, the impact can be varied:

1. Substandard and falsified medical products may cause harm to patients and fail to treat the diseases for which they were intended.
2. They lead to loss of confidence in medicines, healthcare providers and health systems.
3. They affect every region of the world.
4. Substandard and falsified medical products from all main therapeutic categories have been reported to the WHO, including medicines, vaccines and in-vitro diagnostics.
5. Anti-malarial and antibiotics are among the most reported substandard and falsified medical products.
6. Both generic and innovator medicines can be falsified, ranging from very expensive products for cancer to very inexpensive products for the treatment of pain.
7. They can be found in illegal street markets, via unregulated websites, through to pharmacies, clinics and hospitals.
8. An estimated one in ten medical products in low- and middle-income countries is substandard or falsified.

Threat to life

The threat to life from counterfeit products impacts many sectors. However, due to the lack of measurement in these areas, it is not feasible to determine the scale of the problem. Some of the counterfeit products that can be life-threatening include:

1. pharmaceuticals and incalculable loss of life
2. transportation parts, vehicles and aircraft
3. spacecraft accessories
4. qualitative links of counterfeiting, funding organised crime and financing terrorism

Europol[43] confirms that since the launch Operation Silver Axe in 2012, targeting the illegal trade of pesticides, 1,222 tonnes of illegal and fake counterfeit products have been seized.

Sector impact from counterfeit products

Although we have only highlighted a few sectors that are significantly impacted by counterfeit products, they affect all sectors. As an example, some common parts and products are used across many sectors.

1. **Steel piping and other steel products** that may not be fit for the customer's design or application. This can cause safety issues for individuals and the environment. Plant failure, unscheduled shutdowns, increased corrosion rates and catastrophic failure, causing harm to plant and personnel, are all risks from fake products.
2. **Fake butt weld fittings** can increase corrosion and lower product resistance, particularly when combined with high temperatures and corrosive materials.
3. **Valves** can include purely manufactured fakes or used valves that have been refurbished and resold by questionable suppliers, which can cause process upsets, downtime and accidents.

---

[43] https://www.europol.europa.eu/newsroom/news/record-number-of-1-346-tonnes-of-illegal-pesticides-taken-market-in-2020-global-operation-silver-axe

4. **Electronic parts.** A rich source of material for counterfeiters is electronic scrap and discarded or obsolete parts, including the interception or acquisition of shipments of end-of-life products disposed of in other countries to avoid environmental regulation. They may represent a hazard if incorporated into critical systems such as aircraft navigation, life support, military equipment or space vehicles.

5. **Semiconductors** are used in a wide variety of critically important applications, such as computers, mobile phones, medical equipment, cars, trains, planes, electric power grids and communications systems. The growth of Advanced Driver Assistance Systems (ADAS) and mapping applications, vehicle connectivity, self-driving cars and electric cars drive the growth of automotive semiconductors. They are usually used, defective and refurbished to look new (and prone to failure).

6. **Chemicals,** including pesticides, have become a lucrative business for criminals. A European study[44] estimates that between 10% and 14% of the EU pesticide market is affected by this illegal trade, with criminals netting up to €70 for every trafficked kilogram of illegal pesticides. Some of the OCGs trafficking pesticides are also involved in other illegal activities, such as trafficking counterfeited cigarettes and illegally trading pharmaceuticals.

Trade in counterfeit and illegal pesticides

The European Crop Protection Association,[45] in outlining how the dangerous trade in counterfeit and illegal pesticides works, described the following area of transportation and routes taken to enter the European Union.

1. Undercover
2. Abusing parallel import licenses
3. Smuggling across the EU external frontier, ready-packed and labelled
4. Importing as ready-packed and labelled products, counterfeiting the proprietary brands and using falsified transport documents
5. Importing as a bulk formulated product with a false declaration or description of the product, to be packed and labelled within the EU
6. Importing as an active ingredient to be formulated, packed and labelled within the EU

Trends in trade in counterfeit and pirated goods

Within the OECD[46] Report 'Trends in Trade in Counterfeit and Pirated Goods' several new areas or developing areas of risk were identified.

1. The propensity of some countries to export counterfeits remains marked by the presence of China (1) and Hong Kong (2), while Turkey (4) gives up its third place to the United Arab Emirates.
2. The companies most affected by the phenomenon of counterfeiting are headquartered in the United States, France, Switzerland, Italy, South Korea, the United Kingdom, Spain and Luxembourg.
3. Companies headquartered in Singapore, Hong Kong and China are becoming targets of counterfeiters, placing them in particularly difficult situations
4. Transit is facilitated by free trade zones (FTZs).

---

[44] https://www.europol.europa.eu/newsroom/news/record-number-of-1-346-tonnes-of-illegal-pesticides-taken-market-in-2020-global-operation-silver-axe
[45] https://www.ecpa.eu/stewardship/counterfeit-illegal-pesticides#section4073
[46] Trends in Trade in Counterfeit and Pirated Goods, OECD (2019)

5. The growing use of counterfeit parcels: 69% of seizures, an increase of six points from the previous report. However, the use of the postal channel is only 11% in value (56% for the marine route).

6. Counterfeit goods that can be hazardous to health, life and the environment are constantly increasing.

Global routes

A company's ability to assess their supply chain for counterfeit product risk is an important part of ensuring that they do not pass on this risk to clients. In assessing vendor supply chains and risk from counterfeit products, there is now a greater challenge with the lengths that criminals go to to hide the original manufacturer and transportation routes. More complex trade routes and methods of transportation are being used, and with the increase in the number of FTZs globally, criminals can use these staging points as an opportunity to hide the original point of departure or introduce business infrastructure to repackage or relabel or falsify manufacture or transportation documentation before onward shipment.

Small shipments continue to grow through postage or express services that are facilitated by the increasing use of online sales via websites or global online marketplace websites. Interpol has issued a warning against fraud whereby people are tricked into buying non-existent medical supplies, making payments intended for medical care into accounts controlled by criminals.

Transit nations

Global organisations such as the Financial Action Task Force[47] (FATF) and the OECD have highlighted the criminal and financial crime risks linked to FTZs. Greater use continues to be made of transit nations and FTZs. They are also used because of:

1. governance and high levels of corruption, poor intellectual property protection and minimum levels of policing
2. FTZs being an enabler for the counterfeit business, offering a relatively safe environment for counterfeiters, with good infrastructure and limited oversight
3. production facilities with low labour costs and poor labour-market regulations, which are an important driver of trade in counterfeit and pirated goods
4. other factors increasing this trade, including low shipping charges; fast, simple and predictable customs formalities; and good-quality trade and transport-related infrastructure
5. trade facilitation policies referring to the fact that enhancing transparency is likely to reduce the likelihood that an economy will export fakes

Global enablers

Examining the enablers of counterfeit products will give us a starting point for procurement and supply chain risk assessment and how to protect an organisation from this global problem.

1. Online purchases and greater use of the postal system is the biggest enabler of consumer purchasing and demand. Additionally, the inability of e-commerce sites to adequately respond to or find effective solutions to mitigate counterfeit product risk allows for the increase in criminal activity.

---

[47] https://www.fatf-gafi.org/media/fatf/documents/reports/ML%20vulnerabilities%20of%20Free%20Trade%20Zones.pdf

2. Lack of awareness in many countries and organisations around counterfeit products and their impact.
3. Motives for the consumption of counterfeit goods include price, easy access and social acceptance.
4. Inadequate sentencing for individuals who are caught and prosecuted for the manufacture, distribution and sale of counterfeit products. There is also evidence that OCGs are turning to counterfeit products because it yields similar profits to drug trafficking, with reduced risk of prosecution or receiving a prison sentence.

Organisational enablers

Some of the common enablers of counterfeit products being introduced into an organisation's supply chain might include:

1. the lack of local availability of original equipment manufacturer (OEM) grade materials
2. poorly defined specification within procurement, which allows for the procurement of low-grade parts or materials
3. no local access to global products
4. the urgent need for replacement of parts or items
5. poor vendor qualification and verification of the supply chain, which would otherwise have identified product risk
6. weak or absent goods receipt and inspection regime, which should have identified suspicious deliveries and counterfeit parts
7. single source or direct award of procurement to a vendor with unreliable or unverified performance
8. an inadequate disposal or obsolescence programme to ensure that inferior products are not reintroduced into the supply chain
9. counterfeit products or non-conformity items that should have had a risk mitigation response being identified
10. attempts to reduce costs, or an organisation that is motivated by the lowest price, creating an environment where counterfeit products are easily introduced into a supply chain
11. limited availability of spare parts suppliers, leading to organisations procuring products from untested sources

Process risk factors

Within organisations, several factors can enable the procurement of counterfeit products.

1. High level of personal discretion and autonomy in decision making
2. Non-transparent or unrecorded decision making
3. Poor organisational compliance with work practices
4. Procedural gaps or disconnected business processes to allow the use of counterfeit products to go unnoticed
5. The lack of ownership or sense of responsibility where risk is identified—what is the strength of the counter-fraud culture?
6. The lack of systematic controls

The use of corruption

Bribery and corruption continue to facilitate counterfeiting, organised crime activities and its supply chain. As examples, bribery of public servants enables:

1. the import and transit of counterfeit products that would have otherwise been seized
2. the issuance of visa or work permits by corrupt officials, which may allow criminal actors to legally establish companies involved in IPR crime
3. a network of brokers and agents to use corrupt practices to infiltrate the legitimate supply chain, especially within distribution and sales
4. bribes to be used to persuade owners of legitimate businesses to cooperate with criminal groups along the supply chain
5. the introduction of vendors who use or manufacture counterfeit products that can be introduced into an organisational supply chain

Forged labels and documents

Documents play a key role in the transportation of counterfeit goods. All ships carrying containers that will enter a country should provide advanced information on bills of lading. This enables customs officials to conduct the necessary risk assessments. To evade the identification of illicit products, criminals use a number of methods to move and avoid identification.

1. Forged documents are used to conceal the contents of the containers or packages.
2. Concealing the point of origin.
3. Adding to products to make them appear more genuine and certified for regulation and safety.
4. Use of false invoices issued for imported goods in declarations to customs. This practice is also used to undervalue their imported products.
5. At the stage of distribution of counterfeit goods, fraudulent retail licences enable the infiltration of the legitimate supply chain.

Importing unbranded items is not illegal and therefore they cannot be intercepted or seized by customs or border agencies. Criminals are aware of legislation deficiencies and work around it by importing unbranded goods and then printing counterfeit trademark labels, which are applied before they are transported and sold.

There can be significant challenges in identifying a counterfeit product. As a counterfeit product can be introduced at any point of the supply chain, any approach to mitigate counterfeit product risk should not only focus on building trusted supply chains but also on a mitigation approach at a local level or organisational level.

CHAPTER 9
Data Collection

Ability to collect data

The connection between investigation and intelligence fields, which includes the identification and collection of data, is integral to the success of any outcomes you wish to achieve, whether it is proving or disproving a criminal allegation made against an individual or company or assessing the level of anticipated financial crime risk within future projects.

Although the use of data is a common practice for many international law enforcement organisations, this approach to corruption and associated financial crime risk isn't necessarily followed within the public or private sectors. In many cases, the expertise involved in detection of risk aren't aware of the relevant sources of data that could be valuable in the assessment of procurement fraud and corruption risk or whether there should be a central information collection point to assess their fraud and corruption risk more effectively and efficiently.

Reviewing an organisation's ability to collect and use its own data can be a valuable tool in building an assessment of the typologies of procurement fraud risk it may be impacted by and also how it is using the various data sources to identify staff, consultant, supplier or other third-party risks and whether there are gaps in the current risk identification and mitigation approach. Do departments that hold this data release it to allow data analysis?

DATA SOURCES AND RISK IDENTIFICATION

To ensure that an organisation can profile its procurement fraud risk, it must first recognise which data sources are important and can be used with other sources of information to analyse and profile risk. Some of these potential sources of data are highlighted below.

DATA ANALYSIS

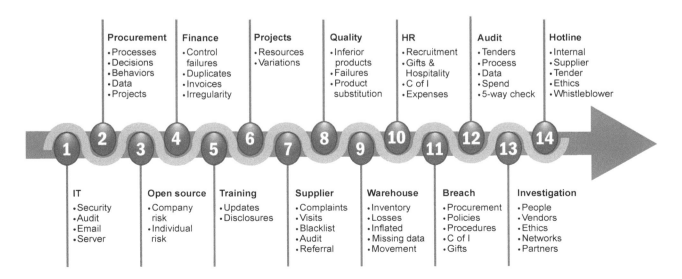

Depending on the size, scale, sector and organisational activities, it may create or retain various types of data. Examples of such data that may be used to analyse procurement fraud and corruption risk might include:

1. Human resources

   Staff data that is retained by human resource departments can be used to check against supplier data or company formation data to verify a conflict of interest. Dependent on the organisation structure data—such as gifts and hospitality disclosures, conflict-of-interest registers and expenses data—may also be held.

   Case study

   During a large infrastructure programme of works, a new contractor was awarded ten low-value contracts of $20,000 each and then awarded larger contracts as their workforce increased. Following bribery allegations, an investigation identified that basic checks of the new contractor—which would have confirmed that the company hadn't existed a week before the award of the first contract—hadn't been conducted and that checks of staff data and possible conflicts of interest would have confirmed that one employee was registered as a shareholder in the company and a second was later given shares for their involvement in influencing the award of the low-value contracts and in their role of identifying new works for this contractor. An initial comparison of staff data with executives and shareholders of the company would have established the conflict-of-interest risk. Additionally, a company formation check would also have confirmed that it was less than a week old and didn't have any financial standing or resources.

2. Procurement and suppliers

   In addition to the analysis of procurement data—including procurement card spend and a comparison of data on new vendors with current suppliers to check for any conflict of interest or bid rigging risk—supplier onboarding data can also be referred to during the lifetime of a contract where fraud or corruption risk is identified, to ascertain whether the current fraud is linked to the corrupt award of the contract. Additionally, the monitoring of the procurement route taken against the value of a contract, or the number of responses received during a tender process, may identify fraud or corruption risk indicators.

   Case study

   In their attempt to create the appearance of competition within the tender process, a spare-parts company created a second company that had no products or staff but was used by them to give the appearance of competition in an area where there were limited suppliers. Checks of ownership for each company at the vendor-vetting stage would have identified that they were the same person.

3. Ethics and business conduct

   Having a strong compliance programme is an important part of profiling organisational risk, where data collected on instances of procurement, ethics and financial policy breach may provide additional data that identifies corruption risk within the organisation. Additional data sources might include abuse of travel expenses and petty cash, non-disclosure of conflicts of interest and breaches of confidentiality.

   Case study

   As part of supplier relationship management, a procurement team had meetings with a number of suppliers to discuss potential future projects. On several occasions they held the meeting off-site at different restaurants or cafés. The meals on several occasions were paid for by the supplier and on a number of these instances the meals weren't recorded in the hospitality register. In one company, two of its directors left and stole equipment to help them set up their own company. They bid for work on which their previous employer also bid, and when they won the tender and were awarded the contract, their previous employer made a complaint to the police of theft, including bribery and corruption in the contract award. Although it was later established that there was no substance to the bribery and corruption allegation, staff involved in the meetings where the hospitality wasn't documented were suspended pending the results of the investigation.

4. Security

Protection of commercial data is an important part of an anti-corruption or counter procurement fraud strategy, including preventing data leaks. Breaches of physical or information security, including the security of the tender process, can add weight to the overall analysis of organisational risk. Data retained and collected from security vetting, access and control, and email and mobile data, including penetration testing, can add value to the overall risk picture.

Case study

Following suspicions of corruption, an individual's company emails were secured and monitored. Analysis of his sent emails identified that he shared pricing information with a vendor to ensure that they underbid other companies in future tenders. Further checks of the national business registration database confirmed that the member of staff sharing information was a shareholder of the supplier.

5. Finance

Ongoing analysis of financial data is an important part of detection, testing controls and assessing the common methodologies of procurement fraud, corruption and the diversion of payments.

Case study

An allegation was received that an individual was requesting bribes from vendors to assist them in obtaining single source contracts. Following a whistleblower report from a vendor, an investigation commenced that included the analysis of financial data. This analysis identified that supplier bank account details were being changed regularly to personal bank accounts, then payments were diverted to these accounts and then the accounts were changed back to the original account details.

6. Supplier complaints

Although this may not be the normal route in which suspicions of procurement fraud can be reported, it is not uncommon for competing suppliers to identify and report irregularity within the tender process.

Case study

On a large infrastructure programme of works, a new vendor was introduced and awarded work without any vetting. Other contractors recognised very quickly that they had an improper relationship with a civil engineer and because of his close relationship with the procurement team had influenced the award of single source contracts to this new contractor. A report was made as part of the vendor reporting system about this suspected corrupt relationship and a subsequent investigation identified that the company was set up to illicitly obtain contracts.

7. Whistleblower hotline

A whistleblower hotline can be one of the key areas in which procurement fraud and corruption reports are received. Being able to collect these reports and analyse them against company data can be an important part of building a profile of the reported risk or the scale of a problem.

Case study

An anonymous report was received by an organisation, with a photograph of a personal cheque made out to a supplier from a member of a company's procurement team. Examination of vendor procurement identified that the company concerned was a new supplier, and a review of vendor registration records identified that the procurement staff member had also registered a new vendor, and it was further established that he was named as a partner in the national business register, with the other supplier owner as partner in this new company. The cheque was provided to the supplier and new partner for company set-up costs.

8. Asset management

Asset misappropriation can cause significant financial loss to an organisation, the analysis of goods receipts, asset registers and the movement of assets, including the monitoring of asset loss, write-offs, damage and obsolescence, which are areas that can go unnoticed and hide significant theft and fraud.

Case study

A department set up to dispose of organisation assets recovered over $100 million annually, and an individual working within this department deliberately undervalued and gave away for free high-value and sensitive materials to a company he had developed a corrupt relationship with. He received a kickback of one third of the profit. Items disposed of were compared against current inventory, which identified the extent of the values and age of items disposed of, including the scale of fraud and corruption.

9. Audit

Audit reports can add significant value to an organisation where they are centrally held and shared with interested internal parties to ascertain whether the risks identified within the audit and their root cause are linked to illicit behaviour.

Case study

An audit team was tasked to review single source procurement procedures within a major IT infrastructure project for their compliance. They were not tasked to look at the root cause or potential criminality. The audit highlighted significant discrepancies in the single source procedures—specifically, that the organisation had a single source justification process in place that included a board to assess and approve all single source procurement. In many cases the process wasn't followed, which included minimal or no justification submitted by the project team for the procurement and a large percentage of the approvals by the board not being documented correctly and with minimal information. The audit report had limited distribution and a team who were conducting a corruption investigation into a member of the project team during this period were not aware of the audit or its findings, which may have added significant value and scale to their investigation.

10. Quality assurance

Data collection and retaining records on the quality of materials, including equipment or construction failures, is essential to identify the risk of inferior, counterfeit or substitute products. This information should also be compared against maintenance regimes to assess risk in this area.

Case study

A quality-assurance manager instigated a tender process for a new medical services contract. Due to irregularities in the tender scoring—specifically, that he inserted additional criteria that weighted the scoring to one specific contractor—the tender process was stopped and an investigation of the bidding process took place. It was identified that the current provider of the medical services wasn't invited to bid on the tender, and when asked why they weren't invited to bid for the services, the quality-assurance manager stated that there had been several complaints by members of staff who had used their medical services. He couldn't provide any documented evidence of these complaints or name anyone making a complaint to him.

11. Investigation

Although investigations are usually a consequence of reporting and data analysis, access to current and historical investigation data is important in ongoing analysis and the overall risk profile of an organisation.

Case study

During a fraud, theft and corruption investigation within a global organisation, internal checks were carried out on the individual under investigation and it was identified that they had been investigated several years previously for the same allegations and were dismissed. The individual later applied for a job in the same business area in a different country, but the recruitment department didn't check their internal data sources.

12. Open source

Open-source information on individuals and companies can be a useful tool in assessing a fraud or reputation risk from a vendor, particularly where there is negative reporting, including previous criminal cases. Organisations such as the World Bank publish their debarment list, which identifies the offending company, an outline of their offence or breach of procurement rules, the location of their offence and the country location of the company.

Case study

Several large data disclosures made in relation to offshore accounts over the past few years have highlighted individuals and companies engaged in various crimes, including money laundering. Additionally, a client list of an international agent that offered bribes to develop international business was also released to a national press organisation, which led to numerous investigations and prosecutions of offending companies. Some of these cases highlighted the method of bribery used for the same company in a number of countries.

13. Training

Procurement fraud training is an important part of an organisation's risk mitigation strategy. It is also not unusual, where staff are briefed on the methods of how procurement fraud can be committed, that they recognise risk within their organisation and make disclosures during the training programme. The Association of Certified Fraud Examiners, in its report to the Nations, confirmed that organisations that have formal fraud training are an additional 19% more likely to receive tips through formal reporting mechanisms.

Case study

During a training course given to the executive team of a global oil and gas company, discussions took place around the various methodologies of procurement fraud and corruption and a comparison of the working practices across national operations and projects. A number of risks were identified that included the use of cash to organise events and the lack of consideration for bribery risks when paying government officials for their attendance.

CHAPTER 10
Procurement Fraud Risk Assessment

The planning and creation of a risk assessment are integral parts of targeting and the mitigation of an organisation's fraud and corruption risk. There can be many benefits of risk assessment—at the operational, tactical, and strategic levels—that can assist decision making at the investigation, management, future planning and change management stages within an organisation. Recognising procurement fraud and corruption risk, the typologies and where it can impact an organisation is a starting point to assess the level of risk an organisation faces and the controls it has, or should have, in place to mitigate these risks.

Achieving the best results in the planning stage and introduction of an assessment starts with the identification of available data sources. Incorporating this approach will better enable an organisation to measure the performance of its compliance programmes and the benefits of its risk mitigation response.

This section outlines various areas within a risk assessment that can be considered and when complete can be used to develop an organisation's resources and expertise and controls framework or to drive an organisation's counter-fraud strategy.

Global themes

There are several global themes that should be considered when determining whether an organisation understands the level of risk that may impact it, or in which it may inadvertently pass on risk to clients or partners.

1. Many organisations only use a reactive approach in addressing bribery and corruption risk and only assess risk when it is first identified, limiting its understanding of the extent and impact of unknown risk.
2. In many cases, organisational risk assessment is non-existent, infrequent or inadequate.
3. There can be limited testing of controls in response to identification of risk.
4. Identified incidents of significant fraud or corruption aren't investigated.
5. Many organisations don't have an anti-bribery programme.
6. Organisations can be impacted by both insider threats and external threats.

Value of risk assessments

Organisational bribery and corruption assessments are integral in understanding the level of risk, potential revenue loss and reputational damage that an organisation faces. If the collection and analysis of internal and external data sources are not fully carried out or understood, then there is a likelihood that bribery or corruption risks will go on undetected.

Risk assessment process

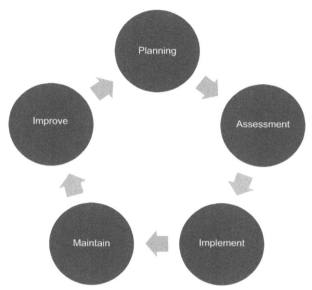

RISK PLANNING

Before any risk assessment that includes projects can be carried out, planning is necessary to put the structure of the organisational risk framework in place to assess the people, process and control risk.

A planning process should be instigated and staffed by suitably qualified personnel. Their purpose is to set out the parameters of areas outlined in the risk framework. The planning stage will assess the key areas of the counter procurement fraud and corruption risk framework, including its implementation.

Key staff should also be identified within each organisation who will lead, coordinate and implement the risk framework within their organisation. This will support the overall coordinated approach and implementation of the organisational or national risk framework, including the ongoing risk assessment process.

Structure

At the planning stage, to implement the framework across an organisation, where relevant, the following information must first be identified and understood. This includes:

1. the relevant organisation to be assessed
2. the size and structure of an organisation, including country and international operations
3. activities of the organisation
4. the supply chain and asset management structure
5. the type and scale of project activity
6. procure-to-pay data management process
7. the organisation's ability to collect, analyse and disseminate data
8. the current counter procurement fraud framework in place
9. the organisation's ability to consistently introduce counter procurement fraud risk frameworks across all relevant areas
10. the ability to assess risk and identify gaps in the organisational risk framework

Procurement fraud typologies

Analysing the data held on cases under investigation, cases closed within the last 12 months and current intelligence held on individuals or company risk will help identify the level of procurement fraud and corruption risk faced. In addition to the normal typologies of procurement fraud and corruption, information held on other typologies, such as theft of data, improper disclosure of information and theft, should also be considered within a risk assessment to determine the corruption and insider threat to an organisation and their associated risks.

Associated financial crime risk

In addition to the crime areas mentioned above, an organisation should also look at any trusted published research or data sources on local, national, international or transnational crime risks that have the potential to impact your organisation or have impacted a specific sector. This can be a valuable exercise in assessing a new risk over the next 12 months to ascertain if the risk of corruption and associated financial crime risks are broader than initially thought.

Stakeholders

Dependent on the sector, industry, partnership or relationship between organisations, there may be a requirement to have input from a number of organisations or stakeholders in the construction of a risk assessment surrounding specific risks. They may have an interest in the completed assessment due to a requirement to implement a response to these risks and the outcomes of the risk assessment.

Risk appetite

Each organisation has a different level of risk appetite that can be described as the amount and type of risk an organisation is willing to accept to meet its strategic objectives. This risk appetite is driven by organisational policy and the subjectivity and decision making of its managers from the information available to them.

In assessing the activity and mitigation against an organisation's risk appetite, the likely impact should be considered within the assessment and mitigation response should procurement fraud be identified.

Considering the risk impact from data collection and analysis, the decision-making process allows an organisation to assess the diverse nature of procurement fraud risk and its potential impact. An organisation can then take the decision to either accept, avoid, reduce or transfer identified risks.

Evaluating the likelihood and impact of procurement fraud risk and the main effects of an associated risk to an organisation should procurement fraud be suspected or detected are highlighted below.

P	**PHYSICAL.** Risk to the health and safety of individuals from procurement fraud including product substitution, product failure, false maintenance regimes
E	**ECONOMIC/ENVIRONMENTAL.** Financial impact from procurement fraud including cost implications. Environmental risks from disposal non-compliance, product failure or inferior quality
T	**TECHNICAL.** Risk to technical performance of capability or equipment from inferior or inadequate products or services
R	**REPUTATIONAL.** Damage to reputation as a consequence of quality assurance, product failure, supplier vetting or criminal consequences of staff, partners or suppliers
O	**OPERATIONAL.** Cost, time, scope and quality implications to current and future operations as a result of identified procurement fraud or corruption
L	**LEGAL.** Criminal, civil, regulatory or contractual implications to the organisation from procurement fraud activity

Although there may be additional areas of impact to consider when making an initial assessment of suspected procurement fraud, common categories that should be considered for procurement risk, particularly within projects, should include:

1. Physical risk
   Different sectors or projects can attract different physical or health and safety risks, particularly where counterfeit or inferior products or works are introduced.

   Case study
   Combat personal protection equipment[48] was identified as presenting a risk of injury due to the cable in the quick release system of the plate carrier being able to separate from the handle, preventing swift removal of the carrier in emergency situations.

2. Economic risk
   The economic risk doesn't just relate to the financial loss from fraud or corruption but could include loss of future contracts, cost of contractual, civil or criminal action, project failures, or infrastructure repairs that require further funding.

   Case study
   Inadequate control measures or monitoring are just one of the situations in which fraud or corruption can be used to introduce additional works or contract variations, where a contractor submits a low bid to win the contract and uses these variations to inflate it to the total cost of a project and increase profits.

3. Environmental risk
   Projects such as infrastructure or construction can have environmental impacts that contribute to climate change and impact local environments and nature and water pollution from various solvents or toxic chemicals.

   Case study
   One of the by-products of drilling for oil can be ground pollution from toxic chemicals used in the drilling process. Remediation contracts are put in place where pollution is identified or to test for this risk. Environmental damage can be hidden through bribery in the contracting process, where the contractor confirmed the completion of the works, where no work had been carried out.

4. Technical risk
   A technical risk can come in many forms, depending on the goods, works or services procured, which might include unknown specification, new technology, inferior quality, maintenance requirements or available expertise.

   Case study
   Since 2004 twelve bridges[49] have collapsed in Italy, and five of these bridges fell between 2013 and 2018 alone. Although it is recognised that a lack of maintenance on public assets that were sold off to the private sector was part of the cause, it is also well published that a number of companies are linked to OCGs that generally use inferior materials and poor contract performance because their goal is to maximise profit.

---

[48] https://assets.publishing.service.gov.uk/government/uploads/system/uploads/attachment_data/file/1046449/Product_Safety_Report_14_01_2022_-_Week_53_v2.pdf
[49] https://www.worldfinance.com/featured/italys-construction-crisis-continues-to-leave-many-questions-unanswered

5. Reputational risk

   A reputational risk is a threat to the positive perception others have, or should have, about a company or its products or services. It is difficult on occasions to quantify the damage caused. However, businesses can go bankrupt from the damage done to the reputation from a product or service.

   Case study

   A global company was prosecuted in a number of jurisdictions for bribery. In addition to the management restructure that was introduced in its attempts to rebuild its reputation, it introduced global anti-corruption initiatives in an attempt to set itself as a global leader in ethics.

6. Operational risk

   The day-to-day running of an organisation and its operational risks might include undermining systems and security or improper management, quality issues and other operational-related errors.

   Case study

   The global pandemic and the rush by national procurement organisations to acquire the limited availability of personal protection equipment meant that many vendors procured PPE from untested sources, and because of this, large quantities of medical supplies and equipment was of an unsatisfactory and inferior specification. This put staff and patients at significant health risk.

7. Legal risk

   Legal risk might occur where there is a potential for criminal, civil or contractual proceedings because of corruption or procurement fraud within a contract or the resulting projects having detrimental outcomes, such as a threat to life, financial loss or environmental damage.

   Case study

   A carpet company that provided services for a regional refurbishment contract of government buildings. An investigation identified that over a ten-year period, it had inflated invoices of approximately 25%. A civil case was taken against the company that also resulted in the company going bankrupt.

Assessing culture

DESIGNING OUT PROCUREMENT FRAUD

Taking the stance that several proactive initiatives take in preventing crime by communicating the message that a person intent on committing fraud or corruption stands a greater opportunity of getting caught because of the risk mitigation in place—giving the actual or perceived view that this is likely to happen—there is a greater likelihood of reducing fraud loss from internal and external sources.

Internal threat

Assessing the governance structures in place within an organisation, including the communications strategy that informs staff and consultants that the organisation takes fraud seriously.

External threat

Communication and engagement with suppliers, so they understand and support the counter-fraud culture and clarify the action their organisation is currently taking to ensure that fraud risk is not passed on.

PARTNERS

Relationship and communication with partners that ensures fraud risks are not passed on, including information-sharing on known and new procurement fraud risks.

ENVIRONMENT

Designing an effective use of physical structures and barriers, including the implementation of security procedures and compliance programmes, to reduce fraud opportunity.

COMMUNICATION AND ENGAGEMENT

An environment that has limited or poor communication and engagement with staff, suppliers or partners can impact its ability to collect available risk information. Examples might include:

1. a lack of engagement or communication with suppliers, which may limit the opportunity for risk identification and reporting within contract or project management
2. where there is limited or no internal and external communication with staff, partners and suppliers, and this may give the appearance that an organisation is not serious about risk mitigation, possibly making it a bigger target for fraud
3. where an organisation does not have education as part of its risk mitigation, limiting the opportunity for staff to recognise and report fraud
4. staff who are unaware of an organisation's counter-fraud policy or do not trust the company's response to incidents, where protecting a company's reputation is more important than investigating the root cause, meaning that staff may not report suspicions in the future and that lessons have not been learned from previous events, so this type of incident may happen again

Vendor counter-fraud system

It should never be an organisation's sole responsibility to mitigate their procurement fraud risk. To verify the potential fraud risk from a new vendor, an assessment of the vendor's counter-fraud culture and mechanisms it has in place is critical in ensuring that any fraud and bribery risk is not passed on and introduced into a contract or project. In communicating an organisational counter-fraud position as part of the onboarding process, clarification should be sought from the vendor of their action in the following areas:

1. An outline and evidence of their counter-fraud governance programmes and the involvement and engagement by its leadership team in identifying and mitigating procurement fraud and bribery risk.
2. Evidence of a vendor's risk management system, that a vendor assesses its procurement fraud and bribery risk and that they have taken steps to mitigate passing potential risks on to their clients.
3. That the vendor has counter-fraud policies and a code of conduct and can evidence that it is published internally and publicly.
4. That the vendor provides counter procurement fraud or anti-bribery training to their staff and suppliers, and if not, that they are agreeable to receive your training before future engagements.

That there is staff engagement in developing the vendor's counter-fraud initiatives and that they have a published hotline and helpline information to provide guidance on ethical concerns.

CHAPTER 11
Risk Assessment Model

Designing a formal model and process for consistent risk assessment can be a valuable method of ensuring that key elements are introduced or considered when creating a risk picture. Organisations may have dissimilar risks or take a different approach to risk assessment, and as such, a risk model should be designed around organisational compliance structures, goals and operational and strategic requirements and engage the relevant individuals, departments and stakeholders who can add value to the overall assessment.

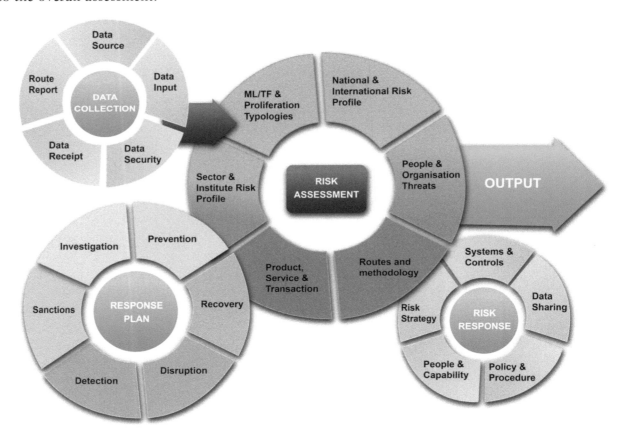

Risk model elements

As outlined above, areas that can drive a risk assessment or may be considered or identified in the planning stage, including gaps within the risk mitigation approach, may be documented within the risk assessment. In developing a risk assessment model, elements that might be introduced are as follows:

1. The ability to identify or collect sources of data that can support building a picture of procurement fraud risk and, where appropriate, identify the challenges of data collection and analysis that may limit the overall risk picture. Does an organisation have internal and external routes in which reports can be made, including anonymously? Does it have the capability and expertise to receive reports and is there security in the reporting process, including protecting the identity of individuals?

100

2. Identifying the typologies and methods of procurement fraud, corruption and associated financial crime risk to be assessed that can impact national or organisational revenues or reputations. Additional areas for assessment might include:

   a. money laundering or terrorist financing links to corruption or fraud risk
   b. national and international risk that might include weakness in national governance or compliance structures or financial crime risks
   c. people and organisational threats, including OCGs, insider threats or offshore business risk
   d. routes and methodologies that might include how the proceeds or corruption and fraud are concealed, moved or placed within a financial institution
   e. products, services and transactions that may be relevant to the type of procurement or projects, including the outsourcing of services
   f. sector and institutional risk, which may be considered where unique crime typologies may impact the sector or institution, possibly including areas such as counterfeit products, bid rigging or weakness in institutional compliance regimes

Tactical Response

The collection of risk data and analysis can be used as part of a tactical response or strategic plan to mitigate risk or respond to identified threats. Areas of a response plan might include:

1. prevention measures used to mitigate the assessed risk, including policies and procedures, systems and controls and expertise and capability
2. detection techniques and expertise available, including audit and data analysis in high-risk areas outlined within the assessment
3. investigation of corruption and fraud cases, including expertise or access to resources
4. financial recovery through contract, civil or criminal law where fraud or corruption is identified
5. disruption of current activities where the level or fraud or individuals engaged in the fraud or corruption is not known
6. sanctioning of suppliers or staff where corruption or fraud is identified within current contracts or contracting procedures

An organisation's strategic approach to risk response might include policies and procedures, systems and controls or people and capabilities in building its expertise to meet the challenges of its internal or external risk.

Disruption

Disruption can be a strategy used in circumstances where significant losses have been incurred. However, it may be difficult or impossible to identify the breadth of illicit activity or individuals involved in the fraud. In such circumstances, leadership may decide to act against individuals or change procedures to disrupt the fraud and prevent continued loss of revenues. The disruptive response is dependent on the area of the procurement life cycle that is impacted. However, some of these responses might include:

1. introducing new policies and reinforcing or updating policies where risk and gaps are identified (this should include enforcing the annual signing of conflict-of-interest and ethics policies)
2. no-notice audits and audits of contracts where fraud is suspected, including financial recovery under the contract

3. introducing policy for change or rotation of staff positions in key risk areas or additional managerial oversight
4. the creation of a committee to oversee bid evaluations
5. introducing a communications strategy and proactive counter-fraud response to highlight an organisation's counter-fraud culture and zero tolerance for fraud and enhance fraud reporting
6. introducing a security review or procedures to identify, stop or change current practices that are non-compliant with organisational policy
7. briefing of staff and suppliers on identified procurement fraud threats
8. communicating to staff that the practice of penetration testing of controls is part of the new control measures
9. publishing actions taken against staff breaching policy to highlight that the organisation takes fraud seriously and is proactive in identifying and dealing with risk

Risk assessment

When developing the assessment of risk within an organisation, there are key elements that should be considered or reviewed:

1. Internal and external trusted sources of information that identify procurement fraud or corruption risk or suspected risk
2. Key stakeholders who can add value to the risk picture
3. Design of risk scoring and matrix
4. An organisation's policies and procedures that support effective procurement and supply
5. An organisation's counter-fraud and compliance policies and procedures
6. The framework that an organisation has in place to prevent, detect and mitigate procurement fraud risk
7. Counter-fraud and corruption strategies in place to coordinate an organisation's approach to risk mitigation and its response
8. Procedures introduced to assess and measure the performance of the risk assessment and an organisation's or stakeholder's response to it
9. An organisation's pre- and post-award contractor sanctions where fraud or bribery is identified

IMPLEMENTING

Once the planning and assessment stage has been completed and gaps have been identified within control measures, procedures, and counter fraud capability, the implementation stage is integral to enhance the current risk framework and an organisation's ability to respond to identified risks. To mitigate the risk identified within the risk assessment, the implementation stage may include introducing or updating:

1. policies and procedures
2. people, resources or capabilities
3. systems and controls
4. measures within the anti-corruption risk framework to close the gaps identified within the risk assessment

To implement the framework across an organisation, where necessary a dedicated compliance group should be introduced with key internal stakeholders who will coordinate the implementation of applicable actions by individuals, departments or capabilities and measure the performance of the mitigation plan implementation.

MAINTAINING

Monitoring the current or updated risk framework is an important part of ensuring that the updating of controls, procedures and counter fraud capability positively impacts the risks identified within the planning and assessment process. Key staff should be identified who will lead, coordinate and maintain the risk framework, and structured communication should be introduced to ensure that the chief executive and risk committee are updated.

MEASURING

Ensuring that an organisation can assess and measure the performance of the counter fraud framework continuously or at planned intervals is essential to its success and mitigation of risk. At the planning stage, leadership and compliance teams should identify key performance indicators (KPIs) that will be used to measure the success of the updated counter fraud framework. Areas of measurement might include:

1. an increase in the number of reports received via an organisation's hotline
2. a reduction of losses within an asset management system
3. the total value of the cases under investigation
4. value of monies recovered under contract, civil or criminal law
5. an increase in identified risks
6. the reduction of non-compliance reports with codes of conduct or policy and procedures
7. feedback from staff, suppliers or partners on counter-fraud culture and approach
8. an increase in the number of protected disclosures

IMPROVING

Whether as part of a management review, annual assessment or external audit, the continual improvement process of a risk framework is integral in ensuring that counter-fraud and anti-corruption measures meet the mitigation requirement of current or new risks. The ongoing review of risk assessment, measurement and improvement of a mitigation response to meet an organisation's risk management requirements that may include reducing the financial loss or reputational damage risk from fraud and corruption.

Types of risk assessment

When contemplating creating a risk assessment, understanding its purpose and end-user requirements is an important part of identifying which data sources to collect and analyse. Three types of risk assessment that may be considered include:

1. operational assessments—used to build a profile and analysis of a specific fraud or corruption risk from an individual, company or group that drives the action necessary to support an investigation
2. tactical assessments—used as a tool to manage the day-to-day resources to target key areas of risk and specific or potential impact to an organisation and to assist management decision making, which might include the introduction of procedures, resources and prevention controls to mitigate financial impact
3. strategic assessments—used to profile the current and future risks that impact an organisation, this type of assessment can be used to measure the adequacy of controls, processes and current resources in place, and the planning in place to mitigate these risks, assisting organisational decision making and change management to protect it from fraud and corruption

Individual risk factors

When considering the factors that can help facilitate fraud—including the counter-fraud environment—**individual**, **process** and **control** risk factors need to be assessed. Some of the common individual risk factors that should be part of the risk assessment include the following:

1. The lack of individual **knowledge** within a current role where there is inconsistency in the training and knowledge of procurement or fraud risk or, as an example, within organisations where the responsibility for procurement lies with each department and the procurement department is seen in a more strategic and advisory role.

2. The lack of procurement fraud **training** within an organisation, which increases the likelihood that it will carry on undetected and unreported.

3. The lack of practical skills and **experience** in key roles and departments, which can provide an environment where controls or processes can be manipulated without being recognised by operating or compliance departments. One of the key points of an insider threat is that the insider knows where the organisation's weaknesses are and how to exploit them.

4. **Pressures** in the work environment, which can also create situations where fraud can go on undetected. An example of this is the excessive workload that can occur within finance departments and the illicit change of bank account details by an insider to launder the proceeds of fraud. The normal process should be for the supplier to provide a confirmation letter on a company letterhead that includes a company stamp and authorised signature. In busy work environments verification of this information can be missed, which allows payments to be diverted to other accounts.

5. Management and **review** of working practices, which are an essential part of an organisation's controls and risk mitigation, so where controls are inadequate there is a greater opportunity, where there is an insider threat, for individuals to commit fraud.
   Inappropriate relationships with clients are not uncommon, particularly where key areas of contact with suppliers are not monitored. As an example, where a vendor is looking for new or additional business with the client, and vendor visits or meetings are not monitored or documented, the risk and opportunity for bribery to be committed are increased. This can be compounded where a vendor has the pressure of sales targets and commission as part of their business model and where there is no guidance or leadership on ethical standards, which may create an environment and opportunity for bribery to be part of an individual's model to meet sales targets.

6. Where an individual has a personal or financial interest with a vendor, which can cause a **conflict of interest** to arise in most areas of the procurement life cycle, and they can influence the award of a contract or post-award contract management. This would include where sensitive procurement or project data, such as project design, competitor bid submissions or financial data, is disclosed to a competing vendor to benefit their bid submission. Conducting conflict-of-interest checks and declarations is an integral part of any risk mitigation framework. The omission of a conflict-of-interest declaration in key roles and areas, such as the tender selection board, can increase the risk of procurement fraud and corruption.

7. The **belief or perception** that procurement fraud within their organisation is not possible, which is not uncommon for executives within an organisation. Whether it is because they trust their staff or they feel that the organisation has strong controls or that the global figures on fraud have been wildly overestimated, such attitudes towards risk without proper assessment can have a significant negative impact on an organisation where fraud is identified, or more likely will go on undetected.

Process risk factors

When we examine process risk factors that may create an opportunity for fraud or corruption, there are several indicators that can highlight these risks.

1. Non-compliance with procurement or compliance policy where an individual has a high level of personal discretion and autonomy in decision making, particularly in the executive role, where decisions or non-compliance with a policy are not challenged.
2. Where there is non-transparent or unrecorded decision making, an environment can be created in which fraud can be hidden.
3. Poor coordination or unethical work practices may not only create an environment where fraud can occur but can also create a culture where fraud is tolerated.
4. Disconnected work processes and procedural gaps can also create an environment where fraud can go on undetected, particularly where departments do not share data on non-compliance with organisational policy.
5. Where there is no sense of responsibility within an organisation, what leadership example and standard does it set for staff to report fraud suspicions and how can an counter-fraud culture be created?
6. Limited oversight in the supplier onboarding process, conflicts of interest and corruption risk assessment where an individual is involved in the vetting of a vendor and also the award of single source contracts.
7. The lack of systematic controls within an organisation, particularly around procurement, finance, quality assurance and projects, can create an environment where fraud can go on undetected. The assessment of control risks is an essential part of risk mitigation.
8. Where an organisation has a high volume of procurement and invoices, including limited capability to check submissions, a situation can arise where invoice payments may be delayed, or proper checks are not carried out to confirm that work has been completed or goods received.

Control risk factors

An organisation should consider control risk factors in key areas of business and in situations where indicators of procurement fraud risk present themselves.

1. An organisation should have a process in place to ensure that controls are enforced, monitored and reported.
2. Where there are excessive defects or quality-assurance reports, checks should be carried out to verify whether inferior, substituted or counterfeit products are being used.
3. Supplier onboarding is one of the key controls within an organisation to ensure that a vendor is not passing on its fraud risk. Obtaining and properly assessing a supplier's credentials and financial standing, experience, technical expertise and ability to complete the contract is a key first step within an organisation's vendor risk mitigation.
4. The manipulation of quality, quantity, resources, time and cost within projects is a common theme, and controls at the planning stage of a project should be introduced to mitigate these risks.
5. Excessive sub-contracting may indicate a supplier's inability to complete the contract or may be used as a route to hide conflicts of interest or bribe payments to staff who are linked to the sub-contractor. Measures should be introduced to ensure that sub-contractors are vetted and approved prior to their engagement.
6. It is common within a programme of works for specialist staff, such as project managers or civil engineers, to overlap on projects. Controls should be put in place to ensure that a supplier is not billing twice for the same individual on different projects.
7. Where poor performance reports are generated on a supplier's ability in completing a contract, checks must be carried out to determine whether this is the first time this has happened to the contractor or if it is known that they have historically been a problem. If they are a new company, checks should be carried out to determine whether there was any irregularity within the onboarding and tender process that allowed the contractor to win the bid.

CHAPTER 12
Prevention Approach

There are many prevention methods that can be introduced to mitigate procurement fraud and corruption risk, some of which will be covered in this section. However, to more accurately identify which control measures should be used, the risk assessment should be scrutinised by relevant departments or, where introduced, a designated compliance group comprised of key stakeholders for decision making and change management.

Global themes

Fraud and corruption can occur throughout the procurement life cycle and by individuals who can influence decision making or manipulate procurement control measures. There are several common global themes where actions facilitate the opportunity of fraud.

1. Oversight and compliance activities in the pre-award stage of procurement can be much stronger compared to the contract management stage.

2. Systems are overridden or there are controls failures where there is a lack of oversight and control testing within the procurement and finance systems.

3. Where there is a lack of segregation of duties between the identification of need, purchase, goods receipt, work completion and payment role, there is a greater opportunity for an individual to create a false requirement or request payment for goods or services that have not been provided.

4. Failure in procure-to-pay controls where the system should identify irregularity or where data is missing to hide the fraud.

5. Lack of a three- or five-way match that includes comparing the requisition, purchase order, invoice and goods receipt and ensuring that the asset is recorded within the asset register before payment is made.

6. Where there is weak or no delegated procurement authority to provide additional oversight of high-value procurement, an individual may avoid the tender process by splitting orders to keep below the financial thresholds that would otherwise require additional scrutiny.

7. Individuals may misuse the single source or direct award of procurement contracts to hide fraud within the process and illicitly award work to a company that they may have a conflict-of-interest relationship with or where a bribe has been offered.

8. It can become custom and practice within an organisation to split orders to avoid the additional scrutiny and bureaucracy of the tender process. However, this practice can also hide procurement fraud, particularly where a corrupt relationship is hidden.

9. Where an organisation has an inadequate asset management system that should manage a purchase from the receipt of the goods, tracking its movement to end-user delivery, there may be a higher risk of asset theft.

10. Organisations that focus on reputation risk can make the mistake of treating the subject and discussion of procurement fraud and corruption as taboo, and not to be discussed within the organisation. This leaves those organisations open to significant and high-value fraud, or where fraud is identified, it is not adequately responded to.

11. Financial controls are integral to the protection of organisational revenues. However, where fraud risk is not understood, areas such as change of bank account details and financial authority levels can be overridden.

Introduction to risk mitigation

Having assessed and profiled an organisation for risk, the next step is to consider risk mitigation and a strategic response. The crime triangle highlights three elements that must always be present for a crime to be committed—specifically, the desire, ability and opportunity. It is acknowledged in crime prevention that an individual's desire to commit a crime can be difficult to determine. However, mitigating an individual's ability and opportunity to commit fraud, and corruption risk, can be introduced as part of a risk mitigation response. A risk of an insider threat may increase where:

1. an organisation appears to be an easy target, where there is no knowledge of fraud risk or they lack the belief that their organisation could be a target
2. there is no counter-fraud culture or attention paid to fraud controls, including communicating an counter-fraud or anti-corruption message
3. an organisation's culture or policies and procedures create an environment where fraud can be committed or go on undetected

As a starting point, three areas should be considered when building an organisation's counter-fraud and anti-corruption corruption framework.

1. As already discussed, an organisation's **environment**, which may include its culture, security procedures or data management and audit that if not in place could help facilitate fraud where such acts may not have been considered by an insider threat had visible controls been in place.
2. Identifying **opportunity** for procurement fraud and corruption within risk areas may assist in the development of controls, including the likelihood and impact should the controls fail.
3. Establishing where the key areas are that may be a **target** and are accessible, what hurdles and capable guardianship are currently in place and whether additional resources are required to mitigate or monitor risk.

Risk mitigation

CAUSALITY

Target of a criminal's desire. What are the **hurdles** and **guardianship** in place.

An organisation's **culture** and its internal and external **communication**.

Opportunity for a crime to be committed.

There are several global themes when it comes to the causality of procurement fraud and why it can go on undetected.

1. An organisation that does not have a centralised capability that facilitates the collection and analysis of risk information.
2. There is no assessment of risk, particularly around high-value projects.

3. An organisation that does not recognise where the relevant data sources are and how to collect and analyse that information or where bureaucratic departments overly protect data sources and don't release information for analysis.
4. Having a strong procurement department and compliance with procurement procedures can mitigate a significant amount of fraud risk. The risk of fraud can therefore increase within organisations that place minimal importance on procurement expertise and integrity within compliance with procedures.
5. No coordinated procurement fraud response or response plan in place.
6. Minimal or no resources or expertise available to respond to procurement fraud suspicions or allegations. It is not unusual that reports are received for initial investigations to be carried out by heads of procurement or legal departments who have no expertise or experience in this area.

THE SEVEN C'S OF FRAUD RISK REVIEW

Where suspicions of procurement fraud are identified, to collect initial information and assess whether a red flag is a bigger risk or to help identify the scale of a risk an initial seven checks should be carried out.

1. Conflicts of interest
   A comparison should be made of staff and supplier data, including directors and shareholders, to identify duplicate information that would suggest a conflict of interest. Additionally, if applicable, a comparison should also be made of supplier data against other registered suppliers to determine whether there may be a further conflict of interest or bid rigging risk.

2. Company formation
   A check of the national business register to verify the company information, including company formation date, directors, shareholders, address and financials. Such checks might assist in identifying whether a company that isn't able to complete a contract was used or whether they were formed shortly before a contract was awarded, suggesting that a contract award was facilitated by corruption.

3. Contract
   An assessment of current and previous contracts should be conducted to determine whether the suspected fraud risk has just happened or an identified fraud methodology has been ongoing for some time and throughout different contracts.

4. Costs and charges
   Assess available financial information under the contract, including invoices and payments, to check for any fraud risk. This might include analysis for patterns in payment, such as double billing and payments just under the tender threshold, and ascertaining that works or services were completed, to test for a fictitious requirement.

5. Communication
   Carry out analysis of communication between supplier, consultant, third parties and staff through organisational email, telephone or other communication documented within contract files, or other documentation, to assess the level of collusion.

6. Compliance
   Where fraud risk is identified within a current contract or project, in addition to verifying the current compliance approach, a review of vendor onboarding and assessment of the procurement route taken, and decision making, can be a valuable exercise in identifying whether there is an insider threat linked to the contractor.

7. Capability

Depending on the type of fraud or corruption that has been identified, which might include poor performance within a contract, evidence should be collected to ascertain and establish whether the contractor is or was ever able to carry out the work outlined in the contract. This might include a visit to the contractor's premises to confirm the scale of their operations and compare this against the tender submission to identify irregularity.

Common procurement fraud barriers

Although each organisation should implement a risk assessment to determine the level of risk mitigation that should be introduced, there are common barriers that can be used across all sectors to mitigate risk.

1. During the onboarding process, confirming conflicts of interest, a vendor's ability to perform a contract and visiting vendors to assess capability and open-source checks to verify any additional risks that they may not have disclosed.
2. Ensuring there are clauses within contracts that include counter-fraud and anti-bribery clauses, competition clauses to mitigate bid rigging risk, audit clauses and confirmation that the use of sub-contractors must be authorised by the client.
3. An introduction of controls within procurement, financial and quality-assurance departments that include segregation of duties, dual controls within financial approvals and change of bank account details, five-way matches before payment and a physical and IT security assessment.
4. The ability of an organisation to receive reports and respond to suspicions or irregularity from staff, suppliers and consultants.
5. Additional procedures within the organisation that include strong recruitment procedures to ensure that individuals with fraud and undisclosed conflict-of-interest risk are not recruited. Where practicable, staff rotation in high-risk positions should be considered to prevent the development of improper relationships with suppliers that can impact the integrity of the organisation and its contracting process.
6. Testing the integrity of the system in key areas of procurement, finance, quality and asset management to ensure that controls are adequate.

Common procurement fraud controls

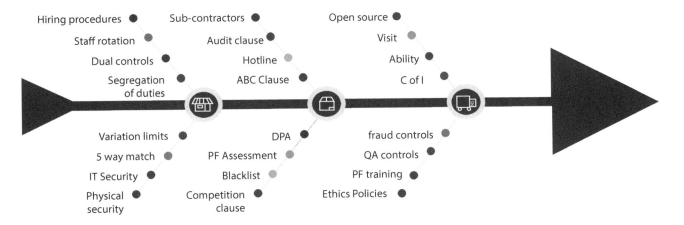

PROCUREMENT SYSTEMS

There are many types of procurement systems that when used correctly have been acknowledged to and can have a direct impact in reducing corruption within contracts. Some of these areas of benefit include:

1. transparency in decision making and approvals
2. reduction of unjustified or unnecessary procurement or projects
3. standardised and simpler bidding documents and procedures
4. increased accountability
5. enhanced efficiency and performance
6. reduced human interaction
7. automation of the tender process
8. increased competition
9. auditability and access to real-time information
10. monitoring of tender process and contract execution

SECURITY ASSESSMENT

Leaks of information, data theft, insider fraud, bribery and corruption have been identified within global reports as some of the highest percentage of risks that executives are dealing with. To protect an organisation's procurement and financial systems in particular, several control measures should be considered that prevent unauthorised access to equipment, installations, material and data, including unauthorised dissemination and tampering with back-up data. Common security procedures might include:

1. Need to know
   The caveat in dealing with all organisational data and its security should be, does an individual 'need to know', and if the answer is no, then access to the data should be restricted.

2. Identification
   The identification of individuals who do not work within restricted areas should be clear, to ensure that access to these areas is limited to authorised staff, ensuring a further layer of security for sensitive data.

3. Office security
   Checks should be made of whether there are enough layers of security within their organisation to protect its people and data from procurement fraud and bribery risk. Building and office security should be a key control in mitigating data theft, and it should include a clean desk policy.

4. Secure storage
   There should be secure storage of hard copy and electronic commercial documents to reduce the opportunity of improper sharing of information.

5. Security procedures
   An organisation should have documented security and audit procedures in place that cover both physical, electronic and data security, including restriction of mobile phones with cameras within procurement and finance departments.

6. Access and control
   In addition to building access and control, the procurement and finance departments should have security access and control to ensure only those with a 'need to know' can enter these areas.

7. Security vetting
   In addition to the vetting of individuals who work within the procurement and finance departments, individuals who work in high-risk positions and can influence the award of

110

contracts should be vetted during recruitment procedures, or there should be additional vetting when they move into a position of higher risk.

8. Security staff
Depending on the type and sensitivity of data, which might include trademark or proprietary information used within projects or procurement, additional physical security and guarding may be necessary.

9. Security audit
Data systems should be auditable, including having controls in place to ensure that data cannot be amended or deleted.

10. Penetration testing
To ensure that integrity within the procurement life cycle remains in place, testing areas that can be impacted by procurement fraud risk should be introduced by internal and external resources.

INTERNAL CONTROL COMPONENT

In designing the prevention and risk mitigation framework within an organisation, areas that should be examined should include the controls environment, risk assessment, controls activity, information and communication, and monitoring activities. Within a counter-fraud environment, additional areas for assessment should include:

1. that an organisation demonstrates a commitment to integrity and ethical values
2. that staff within key roles exercise oversight responsibility
3. that there is established structure, authority and responsibility
4. a demonstration of commitment to competence
5. that accountability is enforced

When constructing a risk assessment, areas that should be considered at the planning stage should include:

1. the risk assessment setting specific and suitable objectives
2. identification and analysis of risk
3. identification and analysis of significant change from previous assessments

On completion of a risk assessment, the introduction of controls activity should include:

1. the selection and development of control measures
2. the selection and development of general control over technology
3. deployment through policies and procedures

When examining how an organisation assesses risk and how this information is used, points to be considered include:

1. that the organisation uses all relevant information
2. that it clearly identifies stakeholders
3. how it is communicated internally
4. how it is communicated externally

Monitoring activities are introduced and used to:

1. conduct ongoing and/or separate evaluations
2. evaluate and communicate deficiencies

Audit approach

The audit of contracts, procedures and control measures is a broad term that depends on the type of works, services or materials purchased and can involve a diverse audit requirement. Many organisations have a planned audit programme. However, where an organisation has a continual risk assessment approach, where new risks are identified, it can allow for a more targeted approach to audit. The targeted audit might include:

1. assessing procurement and project information to identify fraud methodology and financial losses
2. reviewing organisational control measures, roles, compliance activities and process risk, including a counter-fraud framework for control weaknesses

Audit triangle

Research[50] outlining a conceptual framework for an audit triangle that incorporates aspects of governance that emphasises effective internal controls, capable processes and competent personnel assesses how knowledgeable contracting officers are regarding procurement internal controls and what perceptions they have concerning their organisation's susceptibility to procurement fraud.

When introducing an audit into an organisation, there are several areas that should be considered—specifically:

1. that the processes used within the organisation are **institutionalised** and that they are **measured** and continually **improved**
2. that the internal controls introduced by the organisation are **enforced** and **monitored** and their effectiveness **reported**
3. clarification that organisational resources are **educated** and have adequate expertise and are **trained** and have the relevant **experience** in their current role

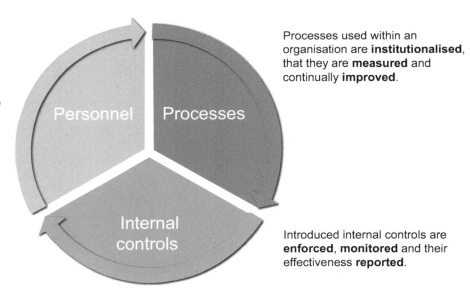

Clarification that resources are **educated** and have adequate expertise, are **trained** and have relevant **experience** in their current role.

Processes used within an organisation are **institutionalised**, that they are **measured** and continually **improved**.

Introduced internal controls are **enforced**, **monitored** and their effectiveness **reported**.

Personnel

Processes

Internal controls

---

[50] Renton and Rendon 2015

Audit control framework

In reviewing an organisation's processes, internal controls and personnel, appropriate and proportionate internal audit activities—or other procedures that inspect contracts, controls and procedures for any indication of procurement fraud and corruption—should be implemented. These include:

1. non-compliance with procurement and financial controls
2. failure by suppliers to comply with the organisation's fraud or ethics policy requirements
3. failure by suppliers to comply with their contractual requirements, giving rise to actual or prospective procurement fraud
4. gaps in controls or implementation of procurement controls

Prevention awareness

For prevention to work, the response must come from the whole organisation. Each individual must understand their role within an organisation's mitigation strategy and there must be clear communication.

PREVENTION AWARENESS

Communication and engagement are an essential part of building a prevention response. Some of the areas that should be covered as part of prevention and risk mitigation include:

1. a published counter procurement fraud strategy that outlines the organisation's approach to procurement fraud and its mitigation
2. internal policies and procedures, such as procurement, being published and enforced
3. staff who are engaged in procurement activities being properly trained, which includes having a clear understanding of the procurement policy
4. as part of the mitigation strategy, a communication plan being created that outlines key areas of communication, responsibility and ownership of an organisation's internal and external communication procedures
5. procurement fraud training being integral for staff working directly or indirectly with procurement and consideration being given to training suppliers at the onboarding stage
6. where an organisation has annual supplier forums, the introduction of procurement fraud awareness around current global threats and threats identified by the organisation being

outlined to suppliers, reinforcing the counter-fraud stance that the organisation takes and, additionally, reinforcing a partnership approach with suppliers to tackle this problem

7. within the published response plan, ownership of the communication plan being documented, including the hotline and reporting process and the role of the designated compliance group

8. an annual ethics declaration being completed and signed by all staff to reinforce the organisation's counter-fraud culture

Training and awareness

When creating and introducing a procurement fraud training programme, an organisation should make its personnel and suppliers aware of and ensure that they understand:

1. the organisation's procurement fraud policy, business ethics and code of conduct, including consequences of any breach

2. the organisation's procurement fraud controls

3. risk to the organisation that can result from procurement fraud

4. procurement fraud indicators and how such fraud can occur

5. methods of reporting procurement fraud concerns

6. the organisation's procurement fraud response plan

7. a supplier's education and awareness of the risks of procurement fraud

8. the need to ensure there is no interference with the operational independence of staff members exercising a procurement function

Communicating policy

When introducing a counter procurement fraud approach, and in building organisational culture, the organisation should communicate:

1. a statement from the executive stating that the organisation has adopted a policy that supports and incorporates the procurement fraud controls

2. that the organisation is implementing procurement fraud controls to give effect to the policy

3. that senior management supports the policy and the implementation of procurement fraud controls

4. that the statement and procurement fraud policy should be communicated to all personnel and suppliers and be published on the organisation's intranet and public website

5. that the organisation should implement procedures under which all appropriate and relevant personnel read the procurement fraud policy and agree to comply with it

6. that records are maintained of all personnel who have received the procurement fraud policy and made the compliance declaration, and that all appropriate and relevant personnel receive the business ethics and code of conduct

Prevention policy and procedures

As part of a risk mitigation strategy, the prevention element is essential in its response to the organisation's risk assessment. Areas covered should include:

1. that the organisation has segregation of duties within key risk areas in the procurement and financial processes, which includes identification of requirement, requisition, purchase, receipt of goods, verifying work or services as complete, and authorisation and payment of invoices

2. as an important part of identifying and managing organisational prevention controls, continuous review of the organisation and project risk assessments, which includes documenting risks within a procurement fraud risk matrix

3. the ability to audit suppliers through contract terms and supplier visits, which is an important part of the counter-fraud message

4. a security review, including a programme of penetration testing in key risk areas of the procurement life cycle

5. monitoring of a contractor's resources, timesheets and invoices within projects, including timesheets and work tickets within facility management contracts, particularly where a high number of personnel or resources are being invoiced for

6. a targeted audit of key risk areas identified within the organisational or project risk assessment

7. continuous data analysis of key risk areas within financial, procurement and asset management within projects

8. the introduction of dual controls in key areas of financial and procurement decision making, including negotiation and payment procedures

9. Delegated Procurement Authority controls being implemented and reviewed on an annual basis

Financial controls

Depending on the size of an organisation and the volume of transactions, the implementation of financial controls should include:

1. a separation of duties, so that the same person cannot both initiate and approve a payment

2. appropriate tiered levels of authority for payment approval, where larger transactions require more senior management authorisation

3. ensuring that the payee's provision of works or services has been approved by the organisation's relevant approval mechanisms

4. requiring at least two signatures on payment approvals

5. implementing a periodic management review of significant financial transactions

6. implementing a periodic or ongoing audit of financial transactions, depending on the volume of organisational or project transactions

7. ensuring that the procure-to-pay controls are implemented and enforced, which includes reconciling the requisition, purchase order and invoice before payment is made

8. ensuring that there is no interference with the operational independence of staff members exercising a finance function

9. introducing a strong verification and authorisation process for supplier change of bank account details

Quality controls

Organisations should implement quality controls, including mitigating risk to the organisation or any of its personnel:

1. from a supplier's use of inferior or substituted goods or services to commit fraud, mitigating risk by an initial assessment of how a supplier mitigates counterfeit product risk within its supply chain

2. by ensuring supplier compliance with regulation and legislation

3. by monitoring suppliers' compliance with quality-assurance requirements, which might reveal the provision of poor quality of goods or product substitution

4. by maintaining auditable records that accurately document quality control

5. by verifying, where practicable, a supplier's ability to monitor their own supply chain and material purchases

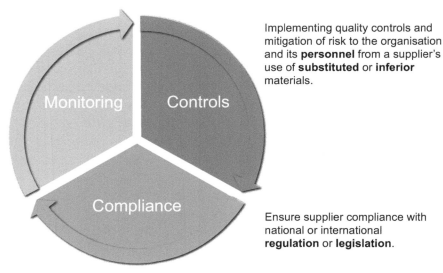

Monitoring a supplier's compliance with quality assurance requirements, maintaining **auditable records** and documenting quality **control measures**.

Implementing quality controls and mitigation of risk to the organisation and its **personnel** from a supplier's use of **substituted** or **inferior** materials.

Ensure supplier compliance with national or international **regulation** or **legislation**.

Human resources

When it comes to areas of anti-corruption and the risk within recruitment, the human resource department is an integral part of an organisation's risk mitigation framework. A number of bribery and foreign corrupt practice cases have highlighted the risk of companies recruiting family members of foreign public officials as an illicit method of obtaining contracts. This type of recruitment may leave a company open to an insider threat, which can include infiltration of company systems and decision making, industrial espionage and exploitation of computer systems.

As part of a prevention response, the human resource department should introduce policies and procedures that not only highlight an organisation's counter-fraud and anti-corruption stance, but also outline its response should a staff fraud risk be identified. These should include:

1. procedures by which appropriate disciplinary action (including suspension or termination of employment) can be taken against personnel who breach counter-fraud and ethics policies
2. implementation of appropriate conflict-of-interest policy, indicating how it will respond to undisclosed conflicts of interest, including closely monitoring and regulating actual or potential conflicts of interest
3. observing restrictions imposed by national legislation
4. not hiring or contracting former public officials in any capacity before a defined period of leaving office
5. conducting due diligence on staff and suppliers where there is a high risk of conflict of interest, including where individuals can influence tender selection and contract award to vendors
6. introducing a policy of rotating personnel who work in high-bribery-risk positions to different positions or roles
7. implementing procedures that provide conditions of employment for personnel to comply with the anti-bribery and fraud prevention policies and give the organisation the right to discipline personnel in the event of non-compliance where personnel pose a procurement fraud risk to an organisation.

Recruitment process

The insider threat and corruption risk are recognised globally as one of the common risk areas that organisations are dealing with, whether it is procurement fraud, theft of data or assets, or unlawful disclosure of information. Although the vetting of new staff will not completely stop the recruitment of individuals who intend to commit fraud or may assist an insider or supplier in illicit acts, such activities can reduce the overall fraud risk. Consistent vetting should include:

1. verifying identity
2. a criminal records check
3. verifying qualifications
4. verifying experience and references
5. credit checks, including bankruptcy or other financial risks
6. conflict-of-interest checks with suppliers and other company links

Asset misappropriation controls

Warehousing and the management and tracking of assets can be a significant area of financial loss through theft and procurement fraud. In addition to having auditable data systems, several control measures should be introduced to mitigate these risks.

1. There should be a segregation of duties around identification of need, requisition, purchasing, payment, and goods receipt.
2. Dual controls should be used where appropriate, particularly around security and movement of assets.
3. Standardised requisition and purchase processes should be used, including a requisition authorisation process.
4. An assessment of security procedures should be conducted when a loss of assets is identified. Automatic write-offs should not be carried out until reasons for the loss are identified and mitigation is put in place.
5. Asset tracking and movement registers are integral in preventing loss and theft of assets.
6. Accurate record-keeping is an important part of asset management, particularly when losses are identified. Analysis of asset data is essential in identifying the point at which losses happen to help introduce mitigation.
7. Having clear policy and procedures, including asset disposal procedures, is integral in introducing a compliance programme within asset management.
8. An annual ethics declaration in areas of procurement fraud risk is an important part of a compliance programme and highlights an organisation's stance on procurement fraud.

ASSET MISAPPROPRIATION

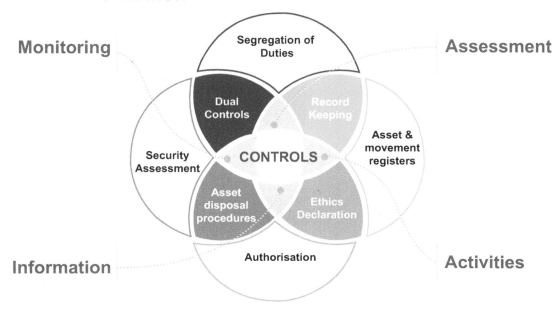

117

Asset tracking

Tracking the movement of assets from receipt to the end-user—or during the lifetime of assets to their final disposal—can in many cases be invaluable in managing and preventing the loss or misappropriation of assets. Actions that should be taken by organisations to mitigate risk might include, where practicable:

1. linking all procurement activity to an asset register
2. audits of asset registers on a predetermined basis
3. information on an asset register including the following details:
    a. identification number or unique reference for the asset
    b. make and/or model
    c. manufacturer
    d. vendor, if different to the manufacturer
    e. date of manufacture
    f. date of acquisition, installation or completion of construction
    g. location of asset

Vetting controls framework

All internal and outsourced staff who are to be involved in the procurement process should be subject to background checks, including:

1. financial checks
2. confirmation of identity and qualifications
3. referee checks
4. criminal records checks

Particular attention should be given to:

1. individuals working within the procurement area
2. those who have influence over the procurement process or access to financial information at a higher-than-usual level
3. any identified or reported conflict of interest
4. any breach of the procurement process or related internal policies by staff who work in risk areas
5. checks being reviewed at determined periods or role changes to ensure that any changes to the information obtained during the background checks are identified (e.g. conflict of interest)

Bid rigging controls

To ensure that there is competition within the tender process and that an organisation limits the opportunity for colluding companies to rig bid submissions, several control measures should be considered.

1. Inserting contract clauses that ensure sub-contractors are approved before use by the main contractor.
2. Expanding supplier lists to enhance the opportunity for competition.
3. Non-collusion certification within vendor bid submissions, including disqualification and disbarment clauses for non-competitive practices.
4. Education of key staff, including tender board, on bribery and collusive bidding methods.
5. Follow up on non-responsive bids.

6. Retention and analysis of pricing, and commercial data on suppliers and products, including historical tenders for the same products.

7. Assessment of current and historical data for patterns of inflated prices by vendors selling the same product or service.

8. Vetting of vendor executives and shareholders to ensure that there are no links between competing companies.

9. Avoidance of unnecessary restrictions that reduce the number of qualified bidders.

10. Monitoring specification or minimum requirement, which may reduce the number of qualified bidders.

11. Greater analysis of pre-qualification questionnaires.

12. Analysis of historical bidding data to assess patterns of contract award or vendors who consistently lose.

13. Creation of links or partnerships with anti-competition organisations.

14. Limit the use of industry consultants within the bidding process, which may create a higher risk of sensitive commercial information being disclosed, particularly in situations where an individual has previous employment links to a bidding company.

Monitoring controls framework

To ensure that there is an effective compliance programme, risk should be continually assessed and additional controls introduced as required. A compliance manager should have in place a mechanism through which they can:

1. monitor purchases and payments made by the organisation to confirm compliance with the organisation's procurement and payment procedures and policies

2. investigate suspicions or allegations of procurement fraud

3. record and report deviations from laid down policies and procedures

4. ensure remedial actions are taken in line with organisational policy

5. record sanctions imposed for a breach of procurement policies and procedures

Management review

A senior management review should be undertaken to establish the continuing adequacy and effectiveness of the procurement fraud controls. This review should be:

1. conducted at regular planned intervals

2. introduced when major changes to the organisation's activities or structures take place

3. documented, and should include key pieces of information, including:

   a. reports of incidents, breaches and control weaknesses that have been identified

   b. a compliance manager's assessment and reports

   c. audits undertaken, including findings and recommendations

   d. reports or statements generated by personnel

Due diligence controls

In addition to confirming a supplier's ability to complete a contract, the due diligence process should establish whether the supplier poses an unacceptable procurement fraud risk to the organisation. Issues that the organisation might find useful to identify include:

1. whether, and to what extent, the supplier has procurement fraud controls in place

2. whether the supplier has a reputation for fraud or has been investigated, convicted or debarred for procurement fraud

3. company verification, which includes verifying that it has a sound financial standing and can deliver the contract and vendor visits to verify the scale of the operation and the quality of goods and materials

4. verifying conflict-of-interest information between vendor, staff and suppliers—as part of these checks, when first registering the vendor's bank details on the system, checks should be carried out for duplicates to ascertain other suppliers with the same details, which might indicate a collusion between suppliers

5. controls and procedures the vendor has in place to protect the organisation from fraud, including within their supply chain, and their counter procurement fraud training programme

6. due diligence, which may additionally include open-source internet searches on the new vendor, its senior executive and its shareholders for financial or reputational risk

7. assessing previous contract performance from third parties or clients

Influencing and manipulating public procurement

The corrupt relationships between OCGs and politicians, senior government or public sector officials to influence the award of a contract is, in many respects, no different to any other corrupt relationship where a business, for example through bribery or cartels, would attempt to influence the award of contracts.

In introducing a response to organised crime risk within procurement—in addition to the normal procurement and procurement fraud controls and compliance procedures that are in place to mitigate the organised crime risk—an organisation must first plan its risk assessment to examine additional areas. These include:

1. individuals in key positions within an organisation who could be a target of bribery from OCGs

2. the types of legal businesses and sectors that can be infiltrated or acquired by OCGs

3. procurement and counter-fraud procedures, including monitoring and compliance

Risk mitigation approach

To introduce an approach to mitigate procurement fraud risk, key areas should be initially considered within any compliance programme.

1. Risk assessing areas of opportunity within an organisation, including control weaknesses, bribery risk and where fraud can be committed.

2. Mapping areas of risk that can be targeted by organised crime and ensuring that hurdles and guardianship are in place to mitigate risk.

3. Building the communication and culture within an organisation to support the identification and reporting of incidents of risk.

It is worth analysing the strategies and methods used by OCGs to influence the allocation of public funds and infiltrate public works[51].

Organised crime partnership approach

The creation of alliances and/or collusive relations with entrepreneurs, politicians and public administrators makes criminals increasingly able to infiltrate government or the public sector. Moreover,

---

[51] http://www.cejiss.org

the involvement of professionals specialising in economic and financial sectors, who provide consulting services to criminals, plays a key role in favouring criminal exploitation of legal business.

Mitigation

In the United Kingdom a new task force has been created dedicated to tackling serious and organised waste crime, such as:

1. dumping hazardous materials on private land
2. falsely labelling waste so it can be exported abroad to unsuspecting countries

The Joint Unit for Waste Crime (JUWC) will for the first time bring together law enforcement agencies, environmental regulators, His Majesty's Revenue and Customs and the National Crime Agency to target waste crime. Only where enforcement agencies take greater steps to share sensitive information with public sector procuring organisations do national procurement systems stand a chance of mitigating OCG infiltration to public procurement.

Supplier onboarding

The first line of defence in detecting and mitigating fraud risk is supplier onboarding. A significant amount of data can be collected and analysed in this area, ensuring that an organisation does not import a fraud risk from a new supplier. There are several checks that should be carried out to verify the risk an organisation faces from a new vendor.

1. Conflict-of-interest checks from the provision of supplier data, including details of executives, shareholders and beneficial ownership, should be checked against staff or other individuals, including PEPs who are involved in the procurement process, including decision making and checking other supplier details for duplicate data to ensure that a member of staff or registered supplier is not linked to the new vendor.
2. Verify that a vendor has conducted this type of work before and has the technical expertise to complete the work. Consideration should be given, where appropriate, to contact a vendor's previous clients to verify their contract performance.
3. Where practicable, a visit to the vendor's premises should be carried out to verify the scale of their operations against those disclosed.
4. Verify a vendor's compliance with relevant legislation or regulation.
5. During vendor visits, are you able to verify the quality of goods and materials, that they will be the same specification required within the contract and that materials will not be substituted?
6. Are you satisfied that a vendor and their management can protect your organisation from modern slavery or child-labour risk in their supply chain?
7. Can you verify the vendor's financial security and ability to complete the contract?
8. Do you compare a vendor's registration date and their formation date before they can bid on or receive work from your organisation? If a company has a recent formation date, has it been set up to commit fraud?
9. Can a new vendor show proactively how they mitigate fraud and bribery risk within their company and supply chain?
10. Does a vendor have their own ethics training or will you provide them access to your training?

Global counterfeit solutions and technologies

Authentication technologies aim to facilitate original product verification and counterfeit recognition by providing solutions that are difficult to duplicate without inviting detection.

1. They are divided into overt technologies[52], visible to the naked eye and authenticated by human inspection (e.g. holograms, colour-shifting ink and watermarks), and
2. Covert technologies, requiring special reading devices for authentication (e.g. security inks, digital watermarks, chemical fingerprints and invisible printing).

Supply chain security

There are many solutions on the market that are used to protect the security of assets in transit and to protect supply chains from the introduction of counterfeit products.

1. Quick response (QR) codes[53] can be used as a low-cost mobile solution that helps enterprises manage and track items with a code attached that documents product information in transit.
2. Radio frequency identification (RFID) tags encoded with an electronic product code (EPC) can be scanned and permanently embedded into apparel products, even woven into textiles, to identify real items against the fakes.
3. The Global Positioning System (GPS) can be used to track information from sensors and send it to a centralised platform, where it is processed to provide users with a view of where their assets or cargo are and provide reports that allow proactive management and security of the supply chain.
4. Authentication technologies include watermarks or serial product identifiers that can be user-verified. Other security features include marks that are only visible under UV light.
5. DNA tags can be highly resistant to UV radiation, heat, cold, vibration, abrasion and other extreme environmental conditions. Manufacturers, brands and other stakeholders can ensure their raw materials and products are protected or product claims are authentic.
6. Tamper-proof or tamper-evident security labels enable manufacturers and retailers to safeguard their brands, increase supply chain security, combat counterfeiting and ensure the safety and authenticity of their products.
7. Holograms remain one of the most secure technologies to fight counterfeiting. Holograms can contain information about the item, such as a serial number or part number, and are resistant to abrasion, high temperatures and tampering.

Independent external oversight

In countries where procurement projects are at high risk from corruption, the impact of this corruption can be varied, which might include poor-quality project outputs or project failure, inferior public services or infrastructure projects that may reduce funding or international support on future projects and ultimately impact national development.

Introducing independent external oversight on projects can be a valuable risk mitigation tool, using expertise in various aspects of project risk—which might include project management, procurement and finance—to monitor and evaluate key stages and documentation within the procurement life cycle, including contract management. Integrity Pacts[54] are an approach used by Transparency International to introduce assessment within the planning and tender stages, obtaining written confirmation from competing and contracted companies not to offer or give a bribe to obtain a contract.

In addition to identifying corruption risk, this approach has been shown to have a number of benefits, which can include identifying bid rigging, inflated pricing and engaging local communities to help identify and report concerns on project implementation.

---

[52] Kwok et al, 2010; LI, 2013; WILSON et al, 2016
[53] https://www.denso-wave.com
[54] https://images.transparencycdn.org/images/2013_IntegrityPactGuide_EN.pdf

VENDOR FRAUD RISK QUESTIONNAIRE

POLICY, PROCEDURE & DECLARATIONS

Does the vendor have counter-fraud and ethics policies?	☐ Yes	☐ No
How is compliance with the policies monitored and managed?		
Have they received, signed and agreed to comply with the organisation's counter-fraud policy?	☐ Yes	☐ No
Do you have a conflict-of-interest policy and register?	☐ Yes	☐ No
Has the vendor made a conflict-of-interest declaration?	☐ Yes	☐ No
Does the vendor have an counter-fraud programme?	☐ Yes	☐ No
Is the counter-fraud programme published?	☐ Yes	☐ No
Does the vendor have procedures for staff and suppliers to report ethics, fraud and bribery concerns?	☐ Yes	☐ No
Does the vendor have an ethics hotline?	☐ Yes	☐ No
Is the vendor's ethics hotline published externally?	☐ Yes	☐ No
Do you have a gifts and hospitality policy and register?	☐ Yes	☐ No
Have you recorded any gift or hospitality given or received from our company staff?	☐ Yes	☐ No
Do you have a procurement policy and procedures?	☐ Yes	☐ No
How does the vendor deal with non-compliance with procurement policy?		
Comments:		

PEOPLE

Have the key executives of the vendor been identified?	☐ Yes	☐ No
Have vendor shareholders been identified?	☐ Yes	☐ No
Does the vendor have any directors or shareholders who are government officials?	☐ Yes	☐ No
Have checks been carried out to establish if any company officers or shareholders are PEPs?	☐ Yes	☐ No
Have the vendor, executive and shareholder details been checked against other suppliers to establish conflict-of-interest or bid rigging risk?	☐ Yes	☐ No
Have the key vendor, executive and shareholder details been checked against staff details for conflict-of-interest risk?	☐ Yes	☐ No
Have the key vendor, executive and shareholder details been checked against national company registers for additional business interests or business risk?	☐ Yes	☐ No
Have open-source checks been carried out on individual risk from executives and shareholders?	☐ Yes	☐ No
Comments:		

COMPANY		
Has the vendor formation date and ownership been confirmed?	☐ Yes	☐ No
Where appropriate, has the vendor been checked against sanctions lists?	☐ Yes	☐ No
Have criminal-record checks been conducted on key executives and shareholders?	☐ Yes	☐ No
Have open- and closed-source checks been conducted on the company, executives and shareholders?	☐ Yes	☐ No
Is there proof of previous works, including vendor references, to confirm performance and ability to complete the contract?	☐ Yes	☐ No
Has there been a vendor visit to verify information provided and the scale of their operations?	☐ Yes	☐ No
Have vendor invoices/inventory been checked to ensure that products aren't inferior or substituted and are to the specification being procured?	☐ Yes	☐ No
How does the vendor monitor and record quality issues surrounding materials provided by suppliers?		
Are you able to verify vendor supply chain security within its operations? This might include manufacture, handling, storage and quality-assurance procedures to mitigate counterfeit and substituted product risk.	☐ Yes	☐ No
Does the vendor have a counter procurement fraud or anti-bribery training programme?	☐ Yes	☐ No
If not, are they willing to complete a training programme before commencement of contract/project?	☐ Yes	☐ No
Is adequate vendor financial information received to establish the ability to complete contract size?	☐ Yes	☐ No
How does the vendor mitigate bribery risk from their suppliers?		
Comments:		

CHAPTER 13
Detection and Data Analysis

Corruption and its links to fraud and other financial crime can impact an organisation throughout the procurement and project life cycle. Developing a counter-fraud and anti-corruption strategy is essential when designing out fraud and corruption risk, and data analysis is an integral part of proactively detecting illicit activity and transactions. Recognising where fraud can happen within an organisation's operations, and the data sources that can identify suspicious activity, is important in profiling an organisation's risk, and identifying the key areas where its people, systems and controls may be targeted is essential in designing a mitigation approach.

Having a common approach to detection and data analysis is essential in building a risk profile for an organisation and outlining its internal and external threats. Where an initial indicator of fraud or corruption is identified, further analysis can be introduced to verify the extent of the risk, its methodology, values lost to fraud, and corruption, including the individuals involved.

An increase in the number of fraud or corruption indicators that an individual or entity is linked to will increase the level of suspicion, which can assist operational decision making to respond to these risk areas. It is, therefore, important that the various areas and types of analysis are understood. An indicator of fraud or corruption risk may be a false positive. Specifically, there may be a simple reason for it. As an example, in situations where there is only one vendor who responds to a call to tender, it may be that the other vendors did not have the time or capability to complete the work. Thus, to positively verify the risk indicator, additional investigations should be conducted.

Planning

The use of data and its analysis is part of the process of proactively building an assessment of risk. Part of the assessment will include evaluating the policies and procedures, people and resource implications, and systems and controls in place to mitigate fraud and corruption risk.

To add value to this assessment, identifying internal and external data sources to support and enhance the analysis can help identify fraud and corruption methodology, including historical, current and future risks that may impact organisational procurement or projects.

To understand how to develop data analysis and where to target these detection techniques, individuals must first understand the typologies of procurement fraud, bribery and corruption and where it can impact the procurement and project cycle. To integrate analysis into an organisation's counter-fraud strategy, a planned approach should be introduced.

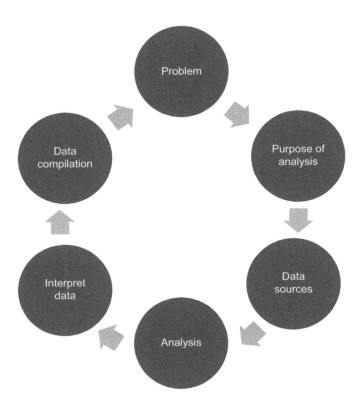

Defining the problem

Where an organisation already has a risk profile that includes areas of identified risk within the procurement and project cycle, this can be used to target detection and analysis techniques. Due to the significant number of fraud and corruption methodologies and the number of sources of data and methods of analysis, where an organisation does not have a risk profile, a planned approach should be taken.

Defining the problems, challenges and process gaps that your organisation has in identifying fraud and corruption risk is the starting point when focusing on where to collect data and introduce data analysis.

Purpose of analysis

Once a problem has been identified—whether it is a threat from contractor collusion, asset loss or weaknesses within the payment system—the purpose of the analysis can then be clearly defined. This could be to identify the level of asset loss due to fraud and theft, corruption risk within the tender process or identifying overpayments or double billing within the payment process. The purpose of analysis, particularly where corruption is suspected, might include:

1. connecting data to insider manipulation of procurement or payment systems
2. network links between decision making, approvals and work completion
3. patterns of collusion between contractors
4. patterns of manipulating procurement routes or tender procedures used
5. weakness, gaps or non-compliance in organisational governance processes, such as analysis of data received from vendors during the onboarding process, for irregularity or risk, such as conflicts of interest
6. data patterns that might include a single vendor response within the tender process or an increased number of false or inflated invoicing within current contracts

Data sources

The next step in preparation for the analysis is to identify the data sources that are relevant to achieve the defined outcomes. Many organisations have departments that retain and protect their data and do not share it with the rest of the organisation. This can have a significant effect on understanding the scale of financial impact from fraud and corruption. Depending on the types of data collected by an organisation, some of the sources might include:

1. finance and procurement
2. quality assurance
3. maintenance and defects
4. asset registers and movement records
5. human resources and vendor onboarding
6. security and system audit
7. compliance data

Common data analysis

Defining the purpose of your analysis will focus your initial approach and identify the data sources required to prove or disprove areas of suspicion. Where there are no specific suspicions of fraud or corruption, and the organisation wishes to proactively assess the level of risk within its procurement of project cycle, a common approach is necessary to help focus finite compliance or audit resources. An initial method might include assessing common risk areas within the procurement life cycle and assessing the strength of an organisation's compliance policies and procedures. These areas might include:

1. single source procurement above the tender threshold or single source just below the financial threshold, which might indicate splitting of requirement to avoid the tender process
2. high-volume or recurring single source procurement for new suppliers
3. only one supplier response within the invitation to tender
4. missing, incomplete or invalid data within vendor registration or procurement system, which might hide the total values of contracts awarded to a supplier
5. over-invoicing or double billing within supplier submissions
6. level of loss within an asset management system
7. renegotiating a contract shortly after its award

Where there is weakness or irregularity identified within the initial assessment of policies and procedures, systems and controls or resources or capability to combat fraud and corruption risk, additional analysis should be conducted to ascertain the level of risk within the identified area.

Vendor onboarding

To assess the conflicts of interest or collusion risk and risk of individuals manipulating the onboarding of vendors to facilitate future fraud, an annual assessment of the supplier onboarding process should be conducted. This information will not only identify whether a company can perform a contract, but it can be used in the initial stages to identify whether a company has been set up or is being used to commit fraud. At the vendor onboarding stage, when considering fraud risk, initial data checks should include:

1. the company formation date compared to the vendor registration date and contract award
2. company financials assessed against the size and value of the contract
3. company management, ownership and shareholder data compared against staff and supplier data for conflicts of interest, fraud and corruption risk

Analysing data for duplicate information is always a good starting point. Checking new vendor data against current supplier data for duplicate entries may indicate either a conflict of interest or collusion between vendors with an aim of:

1. manipulating the tender process
2. corrupt internal manipulation of the onboarding process to commit fraud later
3. the illicit award of single source contracts to a known or fictitious vendor
4. giving the appearance of competition with the use of a fictitious vendor
5. facilitating duplicate billing for the same goods, works or services

To check for conflicts of interest or potential collusive links between suppliers, data that should be analysed for matching details can include names, addresses, telephone numbers and bank account details of staff, consultants or supplier executives, or shareholders.

In situations where an organisation's onboarding process is open to the risk of creating a fictitious vendor, when assessing this area for risk common analysis might include:

1. a vendor with the same or a similar name to a well-known business or brand
2. missing or invalid vendor information
3. incorrect address, company number or VAT number
4. company information not being listed on the National Business Register

Tender process

As a starting point, the procurement route taken—whether it is a single source, restricted or open tender—can highlight an insider threat and whether the type of process taken may indicate a fraud and corruption risk. Types of analysis might include:

1. regular single source procurement in high-value contracts linked to a specific supplier
2. situations where only one bidding company responds in a restricted tender
3. irregularity in tender scoring or additional rating added to a tender matrix
4. comparison of bid submissions to assess for bid rigging indicators that might include the same or similar data from bidding companies

Payment process

The payment process can be manipulated in many ways and can have significant financial impact and loss to an organisation, particularly where there is insider assistance. There are various methods by which fraud can happen and there are numerous detection and analysis techniques to identify the risk. Examples of these risk areas might include:

1. inflating the value of an invoice
2. double billing
3. splitting orders
4. false or inflated work tickets to support false invoices

Procurement data

In addition to the analyses already outlined, verifying and analysing data within an eProcurement system is an important part of assessing the integrity of the system and its usage and applying the various fraud and corruption detection methods to look for risk indicators. Initial steps might include assessing for:

1. missing data
2. duplicate entries
3. incorrect data
4. category comparison to ascertain if a supplier is being awarded works outside of the agreed category

Asset management

An area of the procurement life cycle that in many instances is not given the importance of being a high risk of fraud and theft is the management of organisational assets. It can, if not effectively managed, lead to significant financial loss or theft of organisational or project assets. Common areas of data analysis to detect asset theft or irregularity might include:

1. comparison of data from asset counts and assets recorded
2. assessment of goods requisitions, purchase orders, invoices, goods receipts and asset register (five-way match)
3. pattern analysis for high-value, attractive or regular items listed as lost or stolen backed up by physical checks

Interpreting data

The next step in assessing the risk when you identify indicators of fraud or corruption risk is to determine the value of the fraud or corruption indicator and assess what additional information or analysis will have to be collected to confirm the initial suspicions of fraud or corruption or to prove a false positive and the legitimacy or explanation for a financial transaction.

Data compilation

The final step in building a profile of risk is the collation of the data and its analysis with all other information sources that can either prove or disprove the nature of the suspicions or can be used to identify the method used and link information sources to determine the breadth of an individual's involvement in the suspected crime.

Asset misappropriation

It is recognised by a number of global fraud reports that asset misappropriation is one of the key financial losses that global organisations are dealing with. The proactive element of a risk mitigation strategy is not only valuable in looking for weaknesses in organisational controls, but also in identifying suspicions of procurement fraud.

The high values of organisational assets can make its management and warehousing an attractive target for criminals. To identify the level of risk, a proactive approach should be introduced to detect asset misappropriation.

1. Inventory counts to verify the balance between what goods have been received and are on the asset register, what is stored in the warehouse and what has been received by the end-user will assist in confirming the level of asset loss or misappropriation.
2. In addition to normal checks, independent audits should be carried out to verify the level of organisational loss and the integrity within the asset management system, including conducting a five-way match comparing the requisitions, purchase orders, invoices, goods

receipts and asset register to establish the level of loss, the root cause and at which point within the procurement life cycle theft or fraud risk is high.

3. Analysis should be conducted of an asset management system to establish whether there are patterns in the type of losses, including high-value, attractive or high-volume items. Are regular losses of the same item recognised as a fraud risk?

4. Conflict-of-interest checks and declarations should be considered as an annual requirement to establish any inappropriate link with a supplier.

5. Security and monitoring procedures are integral to the protection and prevention of loss. Non-compliance with security and asset management procedures should be centrally reported to assess the level of risk to the assets and detection systems in place.

6. Recording and reporting procedures should also be introduced to highlight and monitor asset loss, which will allow decision makers the opportunity to introduce proactive analysis and detection to understand the root cause.

7. There should be no automatic adjustment of a variance report identifying asset loss until the organisation is satisfied that the root cause has been identified and that any adjustment is justified and documented.

Data analysis

Data analysis is an important part of the proactive detection of procurement fraud risk. An organisation can hold significant quantities of data in various departments that are relevant in analysis to assess an organisation's procurement fraud risk. When analysing procurement and financial data, there is common analysis that may indicate a procurement fraud risk.

1. Duplicate data within procurement and finance may indicate double billing for the same goods, attempts to avoid financial thresholds that would otherwise have required additional authorisation and oversight or opportunity within the financial system where company data is duplicated to receive payments twice for the same purchase.

2. The same values for different services from the same supplier may be an indicator of a fictitious requirement or false or inflated invoicing.

3. Missing procurement and payment data can also be an indicator of a deliberate attempt to hide the fraud, the person involved or the contract it relates to.

4. The percentage of tenders where only one supplier responds can be an indicator of bid manipulation, where an insider has deliberately manipulated the procurement process, or an example of bid rigging, where the competing companies have colluded together to influence contract award towards a specific company.

5. Round sums that would normally be of different or lesser values for products, or the same round-sum values for different works or services from the same contractor, may be an indicator that works or services are fictitious and were not provided.

6. Regular goods, works or services procured just below a financial threshold that if values were placed together would have instigated a tender process and additional oversight. Have orders been deliberately split to avoid the tender process?

7. Analysis of category-management spend to check for discrepancies, such as suppliers providing goods, works or services outside of their contracted category, a significant increase in category spend with a new supplier or decrease in spending from the norm, or expenditure on non-budgeted items.

Tender analysis

Corruption risk within the tender process is recognised as a facilitator of procurement fraud and if controls and proper monitoring and analysis are not in place, it can go on undetected. Common analysis in these areas should include:

1. the advertising period being shortened to limit the number of vendors being able to view the advertisement or produce a bid submission in time—this may also indicate prior notice to the winning vendor
2. evaluation matrix—is it a standard scoring or has additional criteria been added that might influence the award to a specific vendor?
3. increased weight placed on commercial bid submissions to manipulate a bid where a vendor is not technically qualified
4. increased weight placed on technical bid submissions where a vendor has inflated the value of their commercial bid to hide the bribe payment
5. delays in tender selection and award—are there any irregularities in this part of the process, such as re-tendering or awarding a contract to a lower rated vendor?
6. analysis of bid submissions and scoring to test for irregularity
7. companies whose success rate is affected when there is a change in government

Financial analysis

With the external threat to organisations from false or inflated billing, or the internal threats from the manipulation of financial data or controls, the management of financial data should be treated as high risk from fraud and corruption. To this extent, and due to the various methods of fraud, continuous or regular financial analysis should be considered as part of an organisation's risk mitigation. Common analysis should include the following:

1. Supplier bank account changes, including individuals involved in making changes, which can indicate an insider threat, where changes are made to divert payments to personal bank accounts or others involved in the fraud, such as:

   a. vendor invoices being paid into a personal account or an account with a different company name
   b. multiple suppliers being paid into the same single account
   c. missing data, including new bank account details, that limit or prevent tracking of payments received in the system

2. Duplicate bank account details from different suppliers, which may indicate fraud or bribery, where a bribe is laundered through the supplier's change of bank account details.
3. Suppliers with a different bank account name, possibly indicating that a fictitious requirement for goods, works or services has been created to divert organisational funds.
4. Analysis of an individual's activity, such as making suspicious changes within the financial system or an individual requesting the change.
5. Inflated invoices or overpayments being made to a supplier, which is a common method of fraud, where individuals, if caught, can state that it was a mistake and repay the overpayment.
6. Supplier regularly receiving advanced payments without justification. Have the goods, works or services been provided or are they fictitious requirements? Compare against change of bank account details during the period of advanced payments to ascertain whether payments are made into personal or other bank accounts.

Common risk analysis

There are many sources of data an organisation can use to detect fraud risk. Collecting and analysing organisational data can highlight fraud and conflict-of-interest risk. Data sources used to detect fraud risk can include the following:

1. **Name of supplier,** which can be used to compare against other companies with the same or similar-sounding names (as an example, a name similar to a well-known company or brand

that gives it improper credibility). This is a practice that can be used by individuals using or creating ghost companies.

2. **Company number** to check against other suppliers and ensure there is not a duplicate, and to confirm formation date of the company in the national business register.

3. A **company formation** date should be checked against the date of contract award, particularly where a company is unknown, to assess whether the company has been illicitly set up to receive a contract or divert funds from a fictitious requirement.

4. **Executive and shareholder** details can be compared against staff details, including non-permanent staff and consultants, or other supplier information to identify duplicate information that might suggest a conflict of interest, corruption risk or potential collusion between suppliers.

5. A **company address** can be compared against staff and other supplier details to identify duplicate information that might suggest a conflict of interest or potential collusion between suppliers and a member of staff.

6. **Vendor registration** dates should be checked against the company formation date and award of the first contract to assess whether there is a corruption risk with dates too close together.

7. Check **addresses and telephone numbers** of the company and key company executives against staff and other suppliers for duplicate data to test for conflicts of interest or fraud risk.

8. Vendor **bank account** details should be checked for duplication in the financial system against other vendors, and check for change of bank account details in the system and the number of times they have been changed. Where appropriate, checks should also be carried out against staff bank account details to check for corruption risk and the creation of a ghost company.

9. Where fraudulent or other illicit activity is identified within contract management, it may be advisable to verify the date a vendor is **recorded** on the system and whether corruption was used in the contract award process to award a contract to an unsuitable contractor.

10. Identifying who **proposed** the company might indicate other irregular activity and potential conflicts of interest or insider threat.

11. Compare the **product, works or service a supplier provides** against category management details to ascertain whether a supplier has been contracted outside of their services. Have the normal procurement controls been circumvented?

12. Analysis of **spend levels** to assess whether there are irregular patterns that might indicate favouritism of a new supplier.

13. Breaches of contractual requirements or **exception reporting** within projects that highlight what is outside the scope of what is considered a normal range of risk, should be assessed against available data to determine whether reports indicate a fraud risk.

14. **Advanced payments** should be analysed against single source procurement to determine whether there has been misuse of this requirement. Can it be verified that goods or services were provided?

15. **Purchase orders** should be analysed for completeness to ensure that they are not vague to hide the fraud.

16. **Invoice analysis** that includes duplicate invoices from the same supplier and comparison with the contract schedule of rates, requisition and purchase order to verify accuracy of submissions. Where irregularity is identified, the person who raised the requirement or created the purchase order should be identified.

17. Verifying invoices for resources against supplier timesheets, which should be backed up by no-notice onsite visits to verify integrity within supplier invoicing.

18. Comparison of an **asset register** against purchases to identify irregularity in receipt of goods. Have payments been made for goods not received?

19. Analysis of **maintenance records** to scrutinise for fictitious requirements or regular urgent requirements for equipment failures. Is there a risk of inferior or substituted products or a corruption risk with the individual who is creating a false maintenance requirement?

20. Records held on **quality-assurance** reports that, combined with maintenance records, might identify areas of concerns around inferior, substituted or counterfeit products.
21. Analysis of **variations** and **change orders** within projects, including how quickly after a contract signature the first variation is approved, to assess whether fraud and diversion of funds is a risk.

Detection of counterfeit products

To adequately respond to the risk of counterfeit products, a holistic approach should be taken in its prevention and mitigation. Introducing checks at the point of purchase and goods receipt should be an integral part of counterfeit identification.

VISUAL CHECKS

Simple visual checks to verify the authenticity of a product might include the following:

1. Non-conformity reports can be a way to help spot fake merchandise, including addressing the issue of counterfeit certificates. IEC Conformity Assessment Systems are unique in that they contain online databases, which allow immediate verification of the originally issued Certificates of Conformity and/or Testing Certificates. This means that if the certificates cannot be found on these databases, they are not authentic.
2. The appearance of a product, including the incorrect size, serial numbers, weight, colour, texture or dimensions, language, non-OEM, country of origin, old or worn nameplates, different colour of the same part or incorrect packaging or container.
3. The spelling on a product, including incorrect spelling on the packaging or other paperwork.
4. Documents not present or not in the expected format, or there is a lack of original documentation. Missing authentication documentation and signatures, test reports or unusual shipping information.
5. Delivery through unusual or unexpected delivery routes.
6. Format of documentation, including forged certification or technical data not in the normal format, or there is inconsistency in labelling.
7. Altered, incomplete or worn manufacturer's nameplate, model or serial number.
8. Trademarks altered, damaged, incorrect or missing.

DETECTION TECHNOLOGIES

There is an increasing number of technologies[55] that are being used to detect inferior and counterfeit products. The National Aeronautics and Space Administration, as an example, use a number of these technologies that include:

1. X-ray Fluorescence Spectroscopy
   Widely used for chemical and elemental analysis, particularly in the investigation of metals, glass and ceramics. Equipment used to determine the percent composition of solder used on boards, thickness of coatings and qualitative chemical analysis of elements.

2. Destructive Physical Analysis
   A systematic approach to disassemble a component, electronics board or part to test or solve unique problems ranging from contamination issues to metallurgical questions. The results may enhance complex failure analysis and ensure that electronic components are fabricated to the required standards.

---

[55] https://www.nasa.gov/feature/services-offered-at-failure-analysis-laboratory

3. Optical Emission Spectroscopy (OES)
A tool to verify the chemical composition of metals, which can be critical in ensuring the correct alloy is being implemented in the design application for which it is intended. Any iron-, nickel- or aluminium-based metallic samples can be submitted for OES to provide an accurate quantitative analysis.

4. Real-Time Radiography
A useful took in the screening of components, such as batteries. A non-destructive examination of components, assemblies or materials for internal problems that would otherwise go on undetected and could lead to failure.

5. Scanning Electron Microscope
A tool used in failure analyses to examine samples at extremely high magnifications. This examination can find defects, such as metallisation defects and voids, diffusion faults, passivation faults, dielectric isolation defects, internal wires, bond pads and die mounting.

Global response

There are many forms of response by law enforcement, at a national and international level, to identify and mitigate the risk of counterfeit products. Examples of these efforts include the following:

1. The 'In Our Sites' operation that shut down almost a thousand websites selling merchandise online to consumers. The operation involved law enforcement agencies from within and outside the EU, from North and South America and East and Southeast Asia.
2. Europol has supported the Interpol-led Pangea IX—an international operation targeting the illicit online sale of medicines and medical devices—which involved some 193 police, customs and health regulatory authorities from 103 countries.
3. Operation Opson has brought together a number of public- and private-sector agencies to address the threat from food and beverage counterfeiting and fraud. The operation, led by Europol and Interpol, has had several successes, including the seizure of more than 10,000 tonnes and a million litres of hazardous fake food and drink in operations that spanned 57 countries.

Monitoring schemes

Several monitoring schemes help individuals and organisations detect and respond to risk that includes counterfeit products.

1. Yellow Card Scheme
The Yellow Card scheme[56] is the United Kingdom's system used for collecting and monitoring information on suspected safety concerns or incidents involving medicines and medical devices. The scheme collects information on suspected problems or incidents, including defective medicines, those that are not of an acceptable quality, counterfeit or fake medicines or medical devices.

2. ERAI
ERAI Inc.[57] is a global information services organisation that monitors, investigates and reports issues affecting the global electronics supply chain.

---

[56] https://yellowcard.mhra.gov.uk
[57] https://www.erai.com

3. GIDEP
    GIDEP[58] contains information on equipment, parts and assemblies that are suspected to be counterfeit. GIDEP members provide fact-based reports on items received that are suspected to be counterfeit, which allows participating companies to screen their inventories for items that might have been identified as counterfeit.

4. Manufacturers against Product Piracy (MAPP)
    Automotive suppliers support initiative against product piracy[59]. The industry initiative was created to fight product counterfeiting and to share knowledge on all topics related to brand protection. The European Association of Automotive Suppliers (CLEPA) estimates that fake auto-parts cost suppliers between five and ten billion euros every year.

5. World Health Organisation
    The WHO's global surveillance and monitoring system's[60] objective is to work with the Member States in improving the quantity, quality and analysis of accurate data concerning substandard and falsified medical products and to use that data in the better prevention, detection and response to those products to protect public health.

6. Trading Standards Organisation
    The Chartered Trading Standards Institute[61] tackles and disrupts the supply of illicit goods traded through social media sites and operating internet scams, through national trading standards membership of the National Markets Group. They also undertake surveillance work at outdoor markets on behalf of the Intellectual Property Office.

---

[58] https://www.gidep.org
[59] https://www.mapp-code.com/en/home
[60] https://www.who.int/who-global-surveillance-and-monitoring-system
[61] https://www.tradingstandards.uk

PROCUREMENT FRAUD DATA ANALYSIS			
Entry	Typology	Description	Risk/Action
VENDOR ONBOARDNG			
1	Conflicts of Interest	Undisclosed shareholders or company executive position	Compare staff data with Companies House data to assess for conflicts of interest or corruption risk.
2	Fictitious Vendor	Vendor name similar to a well-known brand	Analysis of open and closed sources to determine the credibility of a new vendor.
3	Cartel	Vendor address duplicate	Comparison of new vendor and supplier addresses, including open-source data for company collusion.
4	Fictitious Vendor	Missing or invalid vendor address	Review of vendor information or database to identify missing or invalid information that may suggest fraud and collusion.
5	Fictitious Vendor	Vendor VAT number	Assess data for incorrect or incomplete VAT numbers.
6	Fictitious Vendor Bid Rigging	Post/zip code	Analysis of duplicate or missing data where a same or similar code might indicate potential collusion.
7	Collusive Bidding Corruption	Telephone number the same as other suppliers or employees	Analysis for duplicate data to assess for corruption or collusion risk.
8	Internal Collusion	Adding vendor data without authority audit log	Analysis of procurement system audit logs to ensure that an authorisation process is used for all new suppliers.
9	Corruption	Politically exposed person	Analysis of vendor executives and shareholders to assess links to government officials or PEPs.
10	Conflict of Interest Corruption	Vendor/employee matching	Check for matches or fuzzy matches of vendor, executives and shareholders/employee information.
11	Conflict of Interest Corruption	Consultant/sub-contractor/employee comparison	Check for matches in consultants, vendors and sub-contractors against employees for duplicate information.
12	Bid Rigging Collusion	New vendor and supplier data duplicates	Compare new vendor and supplier data for duplicate information to assess for collusion and bid rigging risk.
13	Collusion Corruption	Illicit adding of vendor to master vendor list	Can vendors be placed on procurement systems without dual controls?
14	Collusion Corruption	Deleting supplier from master vendor list to reduce competition	Can suppliers be deleted from master vendor data list without dual controls?
15	Corruption	Company created to commit fraud	Comparison of Companies House data, company formation date and bid submission date against contract award date.

PROCUREMENT FRAUD DATA ANALYSIS			
Entry	Typology	Description	Risk/Action
VENDOR BIDDING DATA			
16	Collusive Environment	Same vendors submitting bids in numerous projects	Schedule current and historical bidding data for identified colluding company patterns.
17	Bid rigging	Non-responsive vendor to invitation of tender	Pattern analysis of current and historical non-responsive bids. Consider contacting vendor to clarify non-response.
18	Bid rigging	Non-responsive vendor	Pattern analysis of current and historical bids to assess if this is a common practice and pattern of the same competing companies.
19	Bid Suppression	Bidding company withdrawal from bidding process	Pattern analysis of current and historical bids to assess if this is a common practice and pattern of the same competing companies.
20	Cover Bidding	Bids too high, ruling company out of selection	Pattern analysis of current and historical bids to assess if this is a common practice and pattern of the same competing companies.
21	Bid Suppression	Bidding company making too many conditions within bid	Pattern analysis of current and historical bids, including companies linked to bid rigging.
22	Bid Manipulation	Bid sent to unqualified vendor	Analyse bids where vendor continually wins bid to determine whether bidding companies are qualified to compete.
23	Bid Rigging Collusion	Non-responsive bidders	Verify in how many cases there are non-competing vendors, including type of contract/project.
24	Bid Rigging	Tendering company acts as a sub-contractor	Compare company project sub-contractors against tendering companies.
25	Bid Manipulation	Vendor not qualified to complete requirement	Monitor category management for unauthorised change or addition in vendor category.
26	Bid Rigging Manipulation	Manipulation of the bidding process	Annual analysis in which only one bid was received in the tender process.
27	Bid Manipulation	Manipulation of the bidding process	Short response deadlines against number of vendors response. Are there common winning vendors?
28	Corruption	Manipulation of the procurement route	Single source or direct award contract, where values or other criteria would require introduction of tender process.
29	Bid Manipulation Bid rigging	Manipulation of bidding process to ensure only one vendor responds	Percentage of bids where only one vendor responds. Is there a pattern of winning vendors and increased values of category spend?

PROCUREMENT FRAUD DATA ANALYSIS			
Entry	Typology	Description	Risk/Action
VENDOR BIDDING DATA			
30	Bid Manipulation Corruption	Short advertisement/tender response timescales	Short advertisement or bid response timescales against vendor information to identify common bid winners.
31	Bid Manipulation	Short advertisement and bid response period	Comparison of short advertisement or bid response period against single-responsive bids.
32	Collusive Bidding	Significant reduction in bid pricing when a new vendor is introduced	Analysis of historical pricing or commercial bids compared to new bids to ascertain if there is a significant price decrease.
33	Bid Rigging Corruption	Same pricing in commercial bid submissions	Analysis of bid submissions to determine if bidding companies are sharing pricing information.
34	Bid Manipulation Corruption	Extended approach to influence vendor selection	Comparison of long bid submission period.
35	Tender/Award Manipulation	Extended approach to influence vendor selection	Analysis of expected selection period against long bid selection period.
36	Bid Manipulation Corruption	Pricing changed in commercial negotiating process to meet or beat competing bids	Assess price or technical bid changes to equal competing bids to assess whether insider information has been shared.
37	Procurement Fraud	Inflating pricing/costs	Comparison of bid prices against market price, including standardised products.
38	Tender Manipulation	Improper use of restricted tender process	Assessment of the annual percentage of restricted tender procedures used.
39	Tender Manipulation	Improper selection of vendors to bid on contracts	Analysis of the number and types of companies invited in restricted bidding procedures.
40	Procurement Fraud	Improper and excessive use of single source procurement route	Assessment of the annual percentage of single source procurement.
ACCOUNTS PAYABLE			
41	Corruption	Double payment	Using duplicate company names to make duplicate payments.
42	Collusion	Contract price different from invoice value	Analyse and extract non-duplicates from AP data. Examine why figures are different. Consider financial recovery.
43	Collusion Corruption	Split orders	Analyse purchase orders/invoices and authorisation/approval levels for split orders.
44	Collusion Corruption	Financial threshold	Analysis of orders just below the financial threshold that would avoid additional scrutiny.

	PROCUREMENT FRAUD DATA ANALYSIS		
Entry	Typology	Description	Risk/Action
ACCOUNTS PAYABLE			
45	Collusion	Vendor aggregates spend over financial threshold	Analysis of vendor spend data to establish if tender thresholds are being manipulated.
46	Corruption Collusion	Payments diverted	Manipulation of bank account details. Audit of bank details input/update function.
47	Fictitious Works Corruption	Round sums	Check for round numbers (i.e. $10,000) for goods, works or services from same supplier. Are they single source?
48	False Invoices	Annual payment comparison and trend analysis	Compare annual financial data to determine whether there has been significant increase, decrease or consistent payment totals to vendors (new or old).
49	Bid Manipulation	Dormant vendors	Identify whether a dormant vendor is being used as part of the request for quotation (RFQ) process.
50	Collusion Corruption	Regular authorisation of overpayments	Analysis of regular overpayments to vendors to determine if a specific insider is involved or controls failure.
51	Overbilling	Invoices more than purchase order/contract	Comparison analysis between agreed and invoiced amounts.
52	False Invoice Collusion	Invoices received without purchase order	Percentage of invoices received without requisition or purchase order. Have goods been received or services completed?
53	Corruption False Invoice	Invoices paid without purchase order	Percentage of invoices paid without requisition or purchase order. Have goods been received or services provided?
54	Bribe Payment	Advanced payments	Single source supplier payments where procurement is not urgent.
55	Bribe Payment	Advanced payments	Check annual advanced payments against change of bank account details to verify if used to facilitate bribery payment or diversion of funds to personal bank accounts.
56	False Invoices	Inflating invoice amounts	Compare resources on the ground and contractor timesheets against submitted invoices, including scarce resources.
57	Procurement Fraud	Spend analysis	Check excessive spend or number of contracts for a new vendor.

PROCUREMENT FRAUD DATA ANALYSIS			
Entry	Typology	Description	Risk/Action
ACCOUNTS PAYABLE			
58	Corruption	Payment analysis	Analysis of suppliers that are paid early where an organisation's practice is to pay suppliers late.
59	Procurement Fraud	Change of bank account details	Changing vendor details and country of origin of company or two different companies.
60	Procurement Fraud	Change of bank account details	Check for different vendor and bank account name.
61	Procurement Fraud	Creating and diverting payments to personal or other bank accounts	Analysis of quantity of supplier change of bank account details over a six-month period (should be a small number).
62	Procurement Fraud	Missing bank details	Analysis of financial system for missing or incomplete banking information, making it unable to track payments or payee.
63	Procurement Fraud	Wrong bank details	Vendor registered with a different company bank account name in the payment system.
64	Procurement Fraud	Duplicate details	Different vendors registered with the same bank account details.
65	False Invoices	Sequential invoices	Sequential invoice numbers from the same supplier.
66	Double Billing	Work tickets	Same hours billed for on multiple tickets.
67	Fraud and Corruption	Inflating prices	Analysis of year-on-year purchase prices for excessive price increases.
68	Fraud and Corruption	Avoiding tender process	Multiple purchases of the same item/ materials from the same supplier on the same day.
PROCUREMENT DATA			
69	Ghost Company	Duplicate vendor ID	Verify if registered in error or being used for fraudulent payments.
70	Collusion Corruption	Vendor data audit log	Removing vendor data without authority.
71	Asset Misappropriation	Five-way match	Verify requisitions, purchase orders, invoices, goods receipts and asset register records to assess pattern in missing data.
72	Procurement Fraud	Missing data	Analysis of missing data within eProcurement system to determine if deliberate to hide fraud and corruption.
73	Corruption	Categories spend	Analysis of financial data to ensure that vendors are not being tasked for work and invoicing outside of the scope of contract.

Entry	Typology	Description	Risk/Action
	PROCUREMENT FRAUD DATA ANALYSIS		
	**PROCUREMENT DATA**		
74	Procurement Fraud	Delegated procurement authority	Check financial authority limits against contract value and invoices to assess pattern of avoiding oversight.
75	Procurement Fraud	Non-catalogue spends	Check for increased percentage of non-catalogue spend that inflates the prices given by vendors.
76	Procurement Fraud	Non-catalogue spends	Does the cost-plus percentage remain high as the price for goods/materials increases?
77	Corruption Collusion	Categories spend	Check for increased percentage of year-on-year category spends for suppliers. Is there a significant increase outside the norm?
	**ASSET MANAGEMENT**		
78	Asset Misappropriation	High-value items	Monitor high-value items missing or documented as lost.
79	Asset Misappropriation	Attractive or high-quantity items	Monitor for attractive items or a high quantity of the same items missing or being documented as lost.
80	Asset Misappropriation	Missing data	Check for missing data within warehouse and asset management where goods are described as missing or lost.
81	Asset Misappropriation	Write off damaged or obsolete materials	Analysis of disposal process against high-value, attractive or high quantity of items.
82	Product Substitution	Regular reports of quality and product failure	Verify if parts are counterfeit or substituted products by analysing normal failure rates and confirm with the OEM.
83	Asset Misappropriation	Misuse of single source procurement	Compare new materials described as lost against single source procurement.
84	False Invoices	Inventory comparison	Comparison of trucks and equipment charged against inventory.
85	Theft	Inventory comparison	Comparison of invoices against asset register to identify assets and values stolen.
	**QUALITY & QUANTITY**		
86	Product Substitution	Equipment failure	Analysis of equipment failure against warranty dates and counterfeit risk.
87	Procurement Fraud	Maintenance records/quality risk	Comparison of similar, the same and regular maintenance in the same area.
88	Inferior Product	High call-out rate for equipment failures	Assess call-out rates in the same area to determine if an inferior or counterfeit product has been used.

PROCUREMENT FRAUD DATA ANALYSIS			
Entry	Typology	Description	Risk/Action
QUALITY & QUANTITY			
89	False Invoices	Inflated quantities of materials used	Comparison between vendor purchase of materials and materials used and invoiced in projects.
90	Theft	Items purchased for personal or other private use	Comparison of purchases on projects to identify out-of-specification or unusual purchases.
91	False Invoices	Inflating number of loads and volumes	Measuring the number and volumes of loads provided against checks of what was provided.
TIME			
92	False Invoices	Increasing contractor daily hours	Onsite comparison of number of staff and hours worked against invoiced numbers, timesheets and payroll.
93	False Invoices	Overbilling for number of equipment rental days	Comparison of days onsite, days invoiced and rental information from equipment owner.
94	False Invoices	Misuse of urgent requirement to reduce monitoring on resources	Analysis of the regular use of urgent requirement against increase in procurement, resources or assets.
PEOPLE & RESOURCES			
95	False Invoices	Resource overbilling	Over-invoicing of people, resources or other assets compared to what was provided.
96	Overbilling	Invoice with inflated rates	Comparison of rates charged against agreed rates contained within contract for people and equipment.
97	Overbilling	Invoice with inflated rates	Comparison of expertise against agreed rates. Are individuals being charged at a higher rate?
98	Double Billing	Work tickets	Check for the same work tickets being billed for on multiple invoices.
99	Overbilling	Scarce resources	Comparison of number of scarce resources (i.e. project managers) used against contract requirement and number invoiced.
100	Double Billing	Scarce resources being used on other projects	Analysis of scarce resources information against timesheets.
101	Double Billing	Rental equipment used on other projects	Comparison of rental equipment to determine if being used on different projects and being double billed.
102	Fictitious Requirement	Invoicing for equipment not used or provided	Onsite analysis of equipment invoiced and whether it has been provided.

PROCUREMENT FRAUD DATA ANALYSIS			
Entry	Typology	Description	Risk/Action
CONTRACT AWARD & CONTRACT MANAGEMENT			
103	Procurement Fraud	Reducing requirement or contract value to avoid oversight	Check percentage of contracts awarded just below a financial threshold that would otherwise have required additional oversight.
104	Split Purchasing	To avoid tender process and manipulate contract award	Check percentage of contracts awarded just below a financial threshold that were either split or regularly awarded to the same contractor.
105	Corruption	Influencing contract award	Analysis of higher quantities of contracts awarded to the same vendor.
106	Corruption Bid Rigging	Influencing contract award	Check for a higher quantity of single-responsive bids within a tender process that are awarded to the same vendor.
107	Corruption	Misuse of offshore companies to hide bribe payments and fraud	Check the quantity of companies awarded contracts that are registered in offshore jurisdictions.
108	Corruption	Fraud introduced into award and contract management	Comparison of initial estimated contract value against contract award and completed contract values.

CHAPTER 14
Decision-making and Change Management Process

Once all available data has been collected from the planning and risk assessment process, the next step is to introduce a decision making and change management process that evaluates the current mitigation framework in place, including policies and procedures, systems and controls, and expertise and capability, to determine what activities require changing, updating or introducing to mitigate identified risks.

Risk matrix and key recommendations

When the scope and typologies of procurement fraud have been identified, including the areas of the procurement and project processes where fraud risk can arise and the root cause, the next step in the assessment process is the collection of risk information, in a suitable format, that will allow the visualisation of key fraud risks at a glance. Before taking mitigation action, risks should be documented within the procurement fraud risk matrix. This method of recording information not only allows for the management of recommended actions required to mitigate risk, but it can also be used as a briefing tool for an organisation's executive or risk committee. Areas that can be outlined with a risk matrix could include:

1. risk area
2. procurement fraud typology
3. description of risk
4. risk scoring and priority
5. risk mitigation recommendations

Dedicated compliance group

It is recommended that an organisation creates a fraud response plan that defines risk ownership and has a dedicated compliance group (DCG) that implements the plan with documented responsibilities that assist a coordinated response when new reports of suspicious activity are received. There are significant benefits to an organisation in creating a centralised group of key staff to help coordinate an organisation's response to identified or suspected procurement fraud threats.

1. The support to its operational, tactical and strategic response to enhance a risk framework that includes its prevention, detection, investigation, financial recovery, sanction and disruption response.
2. Facilitates internal communication that includes briefing of the executive or risk committee on current risks and their mitigation.
3. Where a new risk is identified, through the DCG it can be assessed against current policies and procedures, systems and controls, expertise, and capability for mitigation where necessary.
4. Where an investigation is commenced following a criminal allegation or suspicion, the DCG should assess whether other elements of the fraud response plan can be introduced without impinging on the investigation's confidentiality and outcomes.

Fraud response plan

Organisational risk may vary, depending on the size, sector, location and global supply chain. However, introducing a standard structure that includes expertise and management who take ownership of the response to identified risks and their mitigation within a dedicated compliance or other decision-making group will help define what proactive approach should be taken in line with the fraud response plan. In documenting actions and responsibilities within the plan, several areas should be considered:

1. Human resources
   Where there are weaknesses in recruitment procedures, an organisation may increase the risk of employing an individual with a criminal background or a conflict-of-interest risk. Ensure that personnel data is made available to check any conflicts of interest, and where a member of staff is suspected of corrupt behaviour, where appropriate determine the disciplinary approach that should be taken and when. Additionally, consider whether sanctions need to be introduced against individuals who breach policy or are identified as committing a criminal offence.

2. Procurement and suppliers
   Understanding the root cause of any fraud is an important part of risk mitigation, and where procurement fraud has occurred, procurement controls should be assessed to determine whether there was a gap or weakness in control measures that was taken advantage of to facilitate the fraud or whether there was a deliberate breach of procurement procedure. Additionally, consider what further mitigation is necessary to ensure that such an event does not happen again.

3. Policy breach
   There can be occasions where breaching policy is part of the criminal's method of operation or that it is an indicator of an individual's unethical behaviour or potential future risk. Ensure that the department that retains data on policy breaches—including procurement and counter-fraud policies or compliance procedures—has up-to-date information and, if relevant to current investigations, make historical information available to the DCG that allows accurate decision making. Additionally, consideration needs to be given to policy review and whether policy needs to be updated or introduced where it currently isn't in existence.

4. Communication
   A communication strategy should be created, where procurement fraud has been identified, that outlines what internal communication—including briefing of executives and creation of reports on circumstances, root-cause analysis, key risks and financial loss—and external communication will be made, including a media strategy.

5. Security
   The insider threat is recognised as one of the top fraud risks by many global organisations. Where a security risk has been identified, such as the unauthorised disclosure of company data or data theft, consideration should be given to the introduction of a security review to assess whether current physical, IT or communication security and procedures are robust enough.

6. Finance
   Financial procedures and controls should be reviewed where procurement fraud that impacts the finance department is identified. Additionally, ongoing monitoring through the analysis

of financial data should be introduced to assess the breadth of the fraud and insider threat risk and whether the identified methodology has been used by other individuals or suppliers.

7. Whistleblower hotline
A whistleblower hotline can be one of the main areas in which suspicions of procurement fraud or corruption is reported. The DCG should ensure that it is adequately publicised and staffed and that all reports are accurately scrutinised by the organisation.

8. Counter-fraud policy
The monitoring of counter-fraud policies, including conflicts of interest, gifts, hospitality and expenses, can add value to the internal fraud risk assessment and the potential for undisclosed relationships with suppliers. Where unethical behaviour has been identified, a review of organisational registers should be introduced, where it is identified that requirements to document conflicts of interest, gifts, hospitality and expenses aren't being followed. Further publication and dissemination of policies may be required.

9. Asset management
Asset misappropriation can cause significant financial loss to an organisation, the analysis of goods receipts, asset registers and movement of assets, including the monitoring of asset loss, write-offs, damage and obsolescence, which are areas that can go unnoticed and can hide significant fraud and theft. Where asset loss has been identified, an assessment of the root cause should be directed by the DCG.

10. Audit
The tasking of audit resources may be initiated by the DCG to assess control failures or analyse data that includes where false or inflated invoicing has been identified and the compliance group is looking to identify the level of fraud or over-invoicing that has occurred throughout the term of the contract and assist in recovering monies from the evidence collected.

11. Quality assurance
Data collected on the quality of materials, including equipment failures, is an essential method of identifying the risk of inferior, counterfeit or substituted products. A briefing to the DCG should outline areas of risk, including additional assessment of impact where counterfeit or substituted products are identified, such as inferior materials used within infrastructure projects, which may create a health and safety risk.

12. Investigation
Although investigations are generally confidential in nature, the compliance group should be updated on key points where policy and procedures, systems and controls or expertise and capability are impacted or require enhancing to ensure that, where practicable, a risk mitigation approach can run alongside the investigation.

13. Legal
An organisation's compliance programme is an important part of identifying ethical risks within an organisation. Where fraud risk is identified, information can be assessed against current compliance reporting. Additionally, a legal or contractual response may need to be considered against individuals or companies involved.

14. Training
Procurement fraud training can be an important part of a risk mitigation strategy. It is also not unusual, where the staff are briefed on the methods of how procurement fraud can

be committed, that they recognise risk within their organisation and make disclosures to managers or organisational hotlines. Where fraud has been identified, additional training in areas of risk should be considered as an action by the compliance group, and the methodology, if new, should be introduced into the training and awareness programme.

15. Change management

One of the key roles of a dedicated compliance group is change management when responding to a procurement fraud allegation. This includes the assessment and updating of controls, policy, resources, training and awareness and the implementation and revision of organisational strategy to mitigate future risks. For this reason, it is necessary to identify the relevant expertise and give ownership to departments to introduce agreed actions and changes as part of the coordinated response to procurement fraud risk.

Monitor and review

To ensure that an organisation continues to sustain and improve its mitigation framework, monitoring and review should be an integral part of the framework's performance management. Areas that should be considered as part of the risk frameworks monitoring may include:

1. whistleblower protection and reports, including protection procedures to ensure there is integrity within the reporting system
2. compliance with counter-fraud policies and procedures and the publication of internal and external communication
3. the flow of risk information within the organisation, including risk registers, to record and report to the executive or risk committee to ensure that mitigation action is assessed and introduced
4. ensuring that appropriate action is taken against non-compliance with organisational policies and procedures
5. creating annual performance indicators for implementation and ongoing monitoring of the risk mitigation framework and strategy
6. continual monitoring and identification of new threats as part of a counter-fraud strategy, future-proofing an organisation from procurement fraud risk by continual improvement of an organisation's mitigation controls

CHAPTER 15
Creating a Risk Mitigation Strategy

The financial impact where it is identified that individuals have bribed or committed fraud to obtain or retain contracts is not uncommon, and several global cases have highlighted the significant costs and reputational damage that can be caused. In addition to these losses, costs incurred from an internal investigation to identify the extent of the criminality, subsequent enforcement action, settlements and suspension or debarment from government contracts can, depending on the size and quantity of contracts—including the scale of the criminality—have a financial impact of millions, if not billions, of dollars.

To protect an organisation from this possibility and assess for ongoing threats, when building a risk profile and an understanding of the procurement fraud and corruption typologies that an organisation faces, up-to-date information should be used to drive an approach to mitigate identified risks. To mitigate risks, a framework structure should be used and a strategic approach introduced to help build a long-term and consistently monitored change management approach.

In drafting a strategic approach, areas highlighted within the previous chapters should be considered, including the pillars outlined below.

1. The results of the planning stage assessment of the current risk framework and the identified mitigation gaps within the financial, procurement, quality-assurance, security and asset management systems.
2. Adding the results of the risk assessment, the assessment model and the procurement fraud typologies that have been identified, including the areas and roles within the procurement life cycle and business systems that have been targeted.
3. Implementing the mitigation requirements will help build an organisation's long-term mitigation approach to risk. Organisations can be different in size, structure and business outputs, and no one approach to risk mitigation meets the needs of all organisations, so creating a framework or model that takes into consideration the decision making and change management process is important.
4. Enhancing the mitigation framework may require long-term planning and a published strategy that should include performance measurement and monitoring of the new approach.

At its core, there are seven areas that should be incorporated within a procurement fraud mitigation strategy in response to any identified gaps or weaknesses in counter-fraud systems and controls, expertise and capability or policy and procedures.

1. **Risk** includes the ability to identify, collect and analyse internal and external information sources and their data management to create risk assessment products that can give a picture of the threats that the organisation may face, support managerial decision making or assist in the creation of strategy.
2. **Investigation** and the reactive part of the strategy, where suspicious activity is identified and action is taken to uncover the extent of illicit behaviour and determine whether legal action is required.

3. **Prevention** is a proactive response to the review and update of roles, controls and monitoring where current mitigation is inadequate or where a new risk is identified and recognising the root cause instigates a review of current controls and compliance procedures.

4. **Detection** can be part of a reactive investigation or the proactive testing of counter-fraud controls, processes or information within an organisation, which might include audit or analysis of procurement, finance, asset management, quality and project data. This can be a valuable tool when directed by the results of a risk assessment.

5. **Recovery** may include having a structure in place where losses are identified through fraud and corruption and recovered by commercial, civil or criminal law.

6. **Disruption** is an approach used in circumstances where significant losses have been incurred. However, it is difficult or impossible to identify the number of individuals and networks involved or the extent of the fraud or other financial crime. In such circumstances, leadership may decide to act against known individuals or change procedures to disrupt the fraud and prevent continued loss of revenues.

7. **Sanctions** are an important part of a risk mitigation strategy that not only act as a prevention activity when communicated at the start of any business relationship, but additionally, through legal activities that include criminal, civil and administrative action, can protect an organisation from future risk.

Risk Mitigation Strategy

Considering the risk impact from data collection and risk profiling, a structured decision-making process allows an organisation to assess the diverse nature of procurement fraud risk and its potential impact, including the planning and response necessary to mitigate the identified risk and the decision to accept, avoid, reduce or transfer identified risks.

Stakeholders

Identifying stakeholders who may have an interest in the outputs of a strategy or in contributing to the seven elements of the risk mitigation strategy, including sharing of risk information and crime methodologies, can be a valuable approach when planning and introducing strategy.

Designing out procurement fraud

In addition to the seven areas identified within the above risk mitigation strategy, areas within the framework and procurement fraud approach that should also be considered as part of the strategy are as follows:

1. Does the communication and engagement with staff, suppliers and third parties build an organisation's counter-fraud culture?

149

2. Is there a standardised risk assessment approach, as highlighted at the planning stage, and a review of what counter-fraud assessment programme is currently in place? This can be particularly relevant for large organisations with many departments, services or connected agencies.

3. Is there a centralised approach to risk response and, where appropriate, coordinated planning, decision making and change management to ensure the free flow of information within an organisation to assist in mitigation action?

4. Measurement and monitoring of the framework and strategy and any action plan that is created to ensure that the objectives for the strategy are met within the required timescales.

5. Introduction of training and awareness to meet the requirements of the risk assessment and strategic approach.

STRATEGIC APPROACH

There is not one specific approach in designing a procurement fraud strategy. However, designing out risk through risk identification and mitigation elements that should be considered in constructing a framework and the introduction of a strategic approach might include the following:

1. Risk assessment
   Where practicable, an annual risk assessment should be carried out to assess the ever-changing fraud and corruption threats and measure the ongoing risk within procurement and associated activities and mitigation procedures to create or update an organisation's risk approach.

   a. Insider threat assessment
      As a growing threat to organisations, collecting data on corruption risk and its links to fraud and other financial crime is an important part of introducing internal controls.

b. Project risk assessment

The type and scale of a project can create many different fraud risks. To identify and mitigate these risks, introducing an assessment process can be a valuable starting point to detect areas, roles or individuals of risk and ascertain which counter-fraud controls are necessary.

c. Vendor and staff due diligence

Robust vetting of staff and vendors at the recruitment and onboarding stages, including establishing how the vendor mitigates fraud, bribery and counterfeit product risk, can be a valuable exercise in reducing the possibility of companies passing on their fraud risk.

d. Procurement life cycle assessment

Assessing the procurement routes and life cycle to establish the risk within each stage of procurement and to ascertain compliance, influence or manipulation of procedures.

e. Policy and compliance assessment

Review of policies and procedures that if not up to date or complied with can increase the levels or opportunity of procurement fraud risk.

f. Security review

The introduction of a comprehensive security assessment, including physical, communication and ICT systems.

2. Gap analysis

Recognising where the gaps are within an approach to mitigate procurement fraud is an essential part of the risk assessment and mitigation process. In many cases the insider will be using these weaknesses to further their illicit activities.

a. Expertise and capability

Having limited expertise or capability in procurement and associated capabilities, such as finance, asset management, quality assurance, security and compliance, can create an environment where fraud can go on undetected.

b. Policy and procedures

Reviewing policies and procedures to identify gaps or non-compliance can be a valuable approach—particularly where fraud risk has been identified—to ascertain whether the current compliance and mitigation approach is adequate.

c. Systems and controls

Are there up-to-date systems, controls and measures in place for the management of procurement, financial and compliance procedures and activities, including the proactive analysis of data to assess fraud risk.

d. Education and awareness

Introducing a programme of awareness and educating staff on procurement fraud typologies can have significant benefits, including the enhancement of counter-fraud culture, preventing non-compliance and fraud risk and increased reporting of fraud or corruption suspicions.

e. Risk register

Documenting identified risks within a risk register creates an approach where regular assessment can be made by a risk committee, with a reporting structure to leadership for decision making and change management where appropriate.

3. Design and planning

The design and planning of the risk mitigation response and framework is an important element in preventing revenue loss from procurement fraud. Implementing a structure and approach that identifies and mitigates procurement fraud risk can differ depending on the size, sector or structure of an organisation. However, there are common areas that should be introduced in all organisations.

a. Financial procedures
    Introducing financial procedures for contractor payments, cash management and expenses, including an approval process and dual controls.

b. Procurement procedures
    Publishing procurement procedures, including a procurement plan, not only defines how procurement will be conducted but also helps identify non-compliance, which may be an indicator of fraud or corruption risk.

c. Compliance procedures
    Ensuring that a compliance regime is in place for continuous or regular review of an organisation's systems, controls and procedures.

d. Quality assurance
    Introduction of a robust quality-assurance system and maintenance regime, where product or equipment failures are checked for counterfeit, substituted or inferior products.

e. Asset management procedures
    A system that records the movement of all assets and includes checks at the point of goods receipt for quantity, quality and specification to test for error or counterfeit products and ensure that during disposal of assets materials are not reintroduced into the supply chain by illicit means.

f. Security procedures
    The design of security procedures that cover both physical and IT security from both internal and external threats, including the ability to audit capabilities for risk.

4. Implementation
    The introduction of a risk mitigation approach or additions to the current counter-fraud methodology that mitigates the identified risk should cover the areas of policy and procedures, systems and controls, expertise and capability. There are a number of elements that could be implemented.

a. Counter-fraud framework
    A structured approach that incorporates areas of communication, compliance, risk and reporting procedures, capabilities and control measures.

b. Counter-fraud strategy
    The long-term plan and approach created to introduce solutions for identified gaps in the current counter-fraud approach and defend against future risks.

c. Communication strategy
    Introduced as an approach to build counter-fraud culture incorporating various aspects of communication and engagement, including internal and external messaging and reporting, education, contract terms and media updates.

d. Designated compliance group
    A central decision-making and change management group of leaders and managers where procurement fraud is suspected or identified.

e. Fraud response plan
    Documented approach where fraud risk is suspected or identified to ensure that all staff, managers and leaders understand their role, responsibility and ownership within the plan.

5. Performance review

A review of the performance measurement within a strategy is an important part of the continual improvement process. Documenting and analysing data that can be used in the assessment process is a valuable tool in keeping the strategy on track.

a. Non-compliance

Collecting information on non-compliance of policies and procedures or systems and controls can assist in the performance measurement of a strategy and give an indication of an organisation's culture and whether it is improving or declining.

b. Risk reporting

When introducing greater opportunities to collect data and increase reporting, using this information where there is an increase or decrease in the number of identified risks or where a new fraud typology is identified can be a valuable indicator in assessing current control measures and communicating information to internal and external stakeholders where appropriate.

c. Audit results

When used in conjunction with a strategic approach and risk assessment, audits can be introduced to target specific areas of fraud risk rather than as part of a general audit programme.

d. Framework structure

Where a new or updated counter-fraud framework is introduced, ongoing measurement and monitoring of its performance is an important part of the risk mitigation approach.

e. Key performance indicators

KPIs measuring the progress of a counter-fraud strategy and the number and areas of performance to be measured will depend on the areas that are introduced or updated.

f. Investigation and response

As highlighted within the risk mitigation strategy, having the investigation expertise and capability is only one part to a strategy. How suspicions of fraud and corruption are responded to within the mitigation approach, including reporting, decision making and change management, are integral to performance measurement.

ANTI-COUNTERFEITING

When an organisation is planning to introduce counterfeit risk mitigation into its operations, a strategic approach and compliance framework that covers the key areas of risk, prevention, detection, investigation, disruption and financial recovery should be constructed. To mitigate the risk and impact of counterfeits, several key areas that will allow for data collection and analysis of risk should be considered.

BUILDING A COMPLIANCE FRAMEWORK

In building an anti-counterfeiting response framework and strategy, an organisation must take a structured response to risk mitigation. Some of the areas that should be considered include:

1. only purchasing **online** from safe and recognised suppliers
2. a **communication** strategy to engage staff and suppliers where risk is identified, including information-sharing on counterfeiting risks and organisational approach to mitigation
3. organisational quality-assurance **reporting** and analysis
4. **destruction** and disposal policy rather than returns policy, so that parts are not reintroduced into the supply chain

5. hotline and reporting procedures, including **blacklisting** suppliers
6. providing **training** and awareness of relevant global and sector threats to key staff and suppliers
7. procuring directly from original equipment manufacturers, where possible, and not through third parties
8. retaining **data** on a supply chain and suppliers for counterfeit parts to build a picture of organisational risk that can allow ongoing measurement of types of counterfeits and which part of the organisation is impacted, to allow for decision making in future procurement
9. verification of vendor **supply chain** during the onboarding process
10. creating an **approved** supplier list
11. enhancing links with **law enforcement** and international anti-counterfeiting organisations that can assist an organisation when counterfeit products are suspected or identified
12. a counterfeit prevention and **response plan** that includes a legal and contractual response

REPORTING

Where applicable, when developing a communication strategy, an organisation should introduce external reporting to an international anti-counterfeiting organisation that can support a mitigation strategy, which may include:

1. organisational reporting procedures
2. avoiding and intercepting suspect counterfeits
3. identifying suppliers associated with suspect counterfeits
4. learning about ways to help an organisation combat the counterfeit components problem
5. reporting procedures to national or international anti-counterfeiting organisations to assist business group members in responding to updated risk or assist in the screening of inventory for counterfeits

ACRONYMS

ACFE	Association of Certified Fraud Examiners
FCPA	Foreign Corrupt Practices Act
DOJ	Department of Justice
SEC	Securities and Exchange Commission
OECD	Organisation for Economic Cooperation and Development
FBI	Federal Bureau of Investigation
OCG	Organised Crime Group
FLEX	Focus on Labour Exploitation
TI	Transparency International
PPE	Personal Protection Equipment
IPR	Intellectual Property Rights
UNODC	United Nations Office of Drugs and Crime
EU	European Union
WHO	World Health Organisation
OEM	Original Equipment Manufacturer
HIV	Human Immunodeficiency Virus
FATF	Financial Action Task Force
JUWC	Joint Unit for Waste Crime
PEP	Politically Exposed Person
QR	Quick Response
EPC	Electronic Product Code
GPS	Global Positioning System
RFID	Radio Frequency Identification
IEC	International Electrotechnical Commission
MAPP	Manufacturers Against Product Piracy
NTS	National Trading Standards
IPO	Intellectual Property Office
IMF	International Monetary Fund
NHSCFA	National Health Service Counter Fraud Authority
GDP	Gross Domestic Product
GIABA	Inter Governmental Action Group against Money Laundering in West Africa

Ingram Content Group UK Ltd.
Milton Keynes UK
UKHW050630180623
423630UK00004B/7